button it up

button it up

80 amazing vintage button projects
for necklaces, bracelets, embellishments, housewares & more

SUSAN BEAL

The Taunton Press

The Taunton Press
Inspiration for hands-on living®

The Taunton Press, Inc., 63 South Main Street, PO Box 5506, Newtown, CT 06470-5506

e-mail: tp@taunton.com

Editor: Erica Sanders-Foege
Copy editor: W. Anne Jones
Indexer: Lynne Lipkind
Jacket/Cover design: L49 Design
Interior design and layout: L49 Design
Illustrator: Alexis Hartman
Photographers: Zach DeSart and Burçu Avsar,
          Myrna Goldware (button photos pp. 6-10), Russell Mott (p. 12)

Library of Congress Cataloging-in-Publication Data

Beal, Susan.
  Button it up : 80 amazing vintage button projects for necklaces, bracelets, embellishments, housewares & more / Susan Beal.
     p. cm.
  Includes bibliographical references and index.
  ISBN 978-1-60085-073-8 (alk. paper)
  1. Button craft. I. Title.
  TT880.B33 2009
  745.58′4--dc22

745.58
BEA   H   8/23/10

                    2008029690

Printed in the United States of America
10 9 8 7 6 5 4 3 2 1

The following manufacturers/names appearing in *Button It Up* are trademarks:
Aleene's®, Aleene's® Fabric Fusion®, Aleene's® Tacky Glue®, Bakelite®, Britex
Fabrics℠, DAP®, E-6000®, Ebay℠, Etsy℠, Fray Check®, Lucite®, Soft Flex®, X-acto®

to Pearl

ACKNOWLEDGMENTS

My first thanks are to my talented friends who contributed such striking designs to the book. A heartfelt thank you to Cathy Callahan, Nancy Flynn, Melissa Frantz, Mariko Fujinaka, Diane Gilleland, Sarah Johner, Amy Karol, Leah Kramer, Christina Loff, Meredith MacDonald, Torie Nguyen, Alicia Paulson, Rebecca Pearcy, Jennifer Perkins, Linda Permann, Christy Petterson, Kristin Roach, Sally Shim, Laura Stokes, Amanda Blake Soule, Kayte Terry, Nicole Vasbinder, and Jessica Wilson for generously sharing their work with me.

Thank you so much to my editor, Erica Sanders-Foege, for all of her help and for once again coming up with the perfect book title, and to my agent, Stacey Glick, for her expertise all along the way. Thank you to Burçu Avsar and Zach DeSart for their gorgeous photographs, and to Alexis Hartman for her marvelous illustrations. Thanks also to everyone at Taunton for creating such a beautiful book with me. A huge thank you to Myrna Goldware and Russell Mott for sharing their wonderful button photographs.

Thanks to my crafty friends everywhere—I'm grateful to be part of such an amazing and encouraging community of creative people who constantly inspire me. And thank you to my susanstars customers and to everyone who reads my work and my West Coast Crafty blog for supporting my endeavors.

Finally, I want to thank my wonderful family: my mother, my brother David and his partner Dawn, my nephew Julian, and my in-laws Paul and Nancy. Most of all, thank you to my husband, Andrew, for his love and support as always, from the first moment to the last. I could never have pulled this off without you! And to my beautiful daughter, Pearl, who was with me every step of the way—this book is for you.

CONTENTS

INTRODUCTION
BUTTON, BUTTON
3

1
A VINTAGE BUTTON
PRIMER
5

2
TECHNIQUES
& MATERIALS
19

3
NECKLACES &
PENDANTS

solo pendant **38**
duo pendant **40**
layered pendant **43**
delicate pendant **46**
spiky button choker **51**
row of buttons necklace **55**
button charm necklace **58**
button link necklace **63**
knotted necklace **66**
covered button necklace **70**

4
EARRINGS, BRACELETS,
RINGS & BROOCHES

button post earrings **76**
button drop earrings **78**
button dangle earrings **80**
cascading button earrings **83**
button hoop earrings **84**
button link bracelet **88**
button charm bracelet **91**

button cuffs **94**
knotted button bracelet **96**
layered button bracelet **100**
button rings **102**
button brooch **104**

5
HOUSEWARES

button magnets **108**
vintage button cafe curtains **111**
button kitchen set **114**
flowered table set **119**
dinner party set **122**
button bath set **125**
embellished button pillows **126**
button decor **131**

6
ACCESSORIES,
EMBELLISHMENTS
& GIFTS

button hair clips **136**
button haircomb **139**
button embellished top **140**
button embellished skirt **143**
buttoned embellished handbag **146**
button embellished market bag **150**
button stationery set **152**
button jars **156**
button holiday decorations **158**
button toys **163**

RESOURCES 166

guest designers **167**
index **169**

BUTTON, BUTTON

Like so many other people, I fell in love with vintage buttons as a child. Both my grandmothers were crafty, and when I was visiting them, I had a chance to play with their jars and boxes of tempting, colorful buttons. I'd arrange them all in a row, or carefully set each one in its own little place—and when I was really feeling ambitious, I'd stitch one onto a doll dress or one of my own T-shirts as an impromptu decoration, or wear one as a pendant strung on sewing thread. My first sewing basket, an Easter present from my mother when I was eight, also started my very own button collection with a few assorted buttons in a clear plastic box. I remember adding to it with great excitement, picking and choosing buttons from castoffs from my dress-up trunk. My aunt's colorful 1960s dresses were a treasure trove, and even my dad's old blazers and vests yielded some pieces in blacks and browns.

When I was in high school and searching thrift stores and antique shops for jewelry bits and vintage clothes, I found plenty of buttons, too: on cards, loose, on vintage coats, or covered perfectly to match a flowered dress someone had so carefully sewn by hand. Over the next decade, I kept using old buttons for my sewing and jewelry projects, and my collection grew. My mother-in-law passed on *her* mother-in-law's sewing supplies and wonderfully mismatched button stash; my aunt scouted new treasures for me at estate sales. And when my husband, Andrew, was in Amsterdam at an outdoor market, he picked up a handful of instant favorites for me— oversized Lucite® buttons in great, unusual colors.

So when I was designing new projects for my first jewelry-making book, *Bead Simple,* I was drawn to work with some of the buttons I'd been saving for so long. Meanwhile, I found new favorites—by the jar at the Rose Bowl flea market, on their original cards at Exclusive Buttons, and one by one online, at fabric shops, and in thrift stores. Now that I've had the chance to work on this new collection—using everything from the tiniest gleaming shell rounds to deep, rich Bakelite®—it has been so much fun to play with buttons all over again.

As you make your own projects from this book, please don't feel like you need to track down identical materials or copy what I've done exactly. After all, no two crafters—or their collections—are exactly alike. And instead of using the most precious pieces from your stash, you can browse your local craft store for fun pieces to use. I hope you enjoy it all as much as I have.

Happy crafting!
Susan

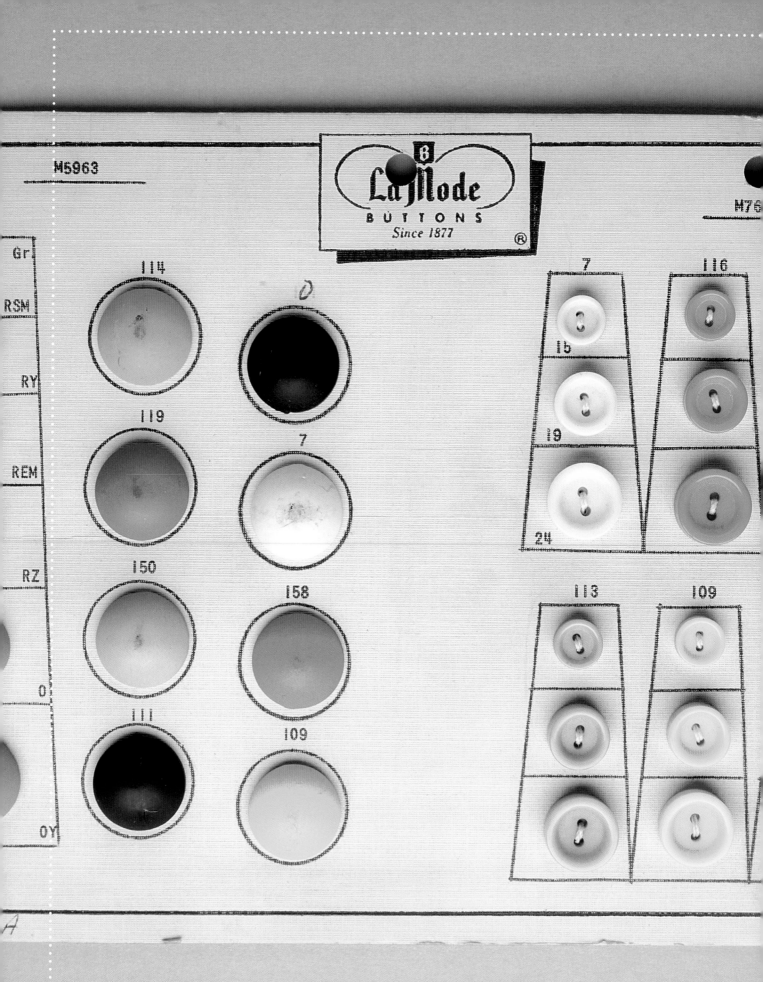

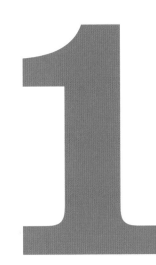

A VINTAGE BUTTON PRIMER

Buttons have long been a subject of fascination for many people, whether their interests lie in making things with them or simply collecting them. The buttons I've used for my jewelry and crafts projects are twentieth century, mostly 1940s, '50s, and '60s (and a few newer). To learn more about them (and see beautiful photographs of every type mentioned here), check out some of my favorite button reference books in the Resources section on page 166.

The earliest buttons came from a variety of natural materials. The very first ones were rough, simple fasteners for clothing worn by people in the Stone and Bronze Ages, most likely made from animal horns. Clay buttons have been found in prehistoric tombs, evidence that they were prized possessions of early man. Later, ancient Greeks and Romans used buttons and loops to fasten their togas and tunics. These early Mediterranean buttons are remarkably similar to our modern drilled or shank styles, though they're blockier and less refined.

Many believe the medieval Crusaders introduced the idea of the buttonhole to Europe as they returned from what now is known as the Middle East. This innovation revolutionized fashion and tailoring, and allowed for a more fitted, sophisticated style of dress.

In the thirteenth and fourteenth centuries, jewelers began creating gold-plated buttons as decorative elements, mostly for men. More elaborate buttons for breeches and waistcoats came into fashion during the Renaissance, and were both ornamental and functional. They were also very expensive, making them well out of reach for most people. In the fifteenth century, Mary, Queen of Scots, and Henry VIII had legendary jeweled button collections. Much later, in the seventeenth century, simpler artisan buttons made of natural materials became widely available.

The First Golden Age

In the 1700s, during what is considered the "golden age" of buttons, they began to be mass-produced so they were available—and affordable—to many for the first time. Increasingly sophisticated methods like engraving, painting, inlay work, embroidery, and other embellishments were in common use. Buttons

PASSEMENTERIE
FABRIC BUTTON
1700s

BONE PINSHANK BUTTON,
LATE 1700s

BUTTON SHOP, GLENDALE AND NASHAWANNUCK IN EASTHAMPTON, MASS.

became tiny canvases to display exquisite art or artistry, tell a story, or reflect an event or an exciting new trend in politics, literature, fashion, or society. Most buttons in today's collections are from the eighteenth century and later, though many of the earliest pieces have been lost to time and reside only in paintings and sculptures from those eras.

Increased international and overseas trading spread buttons far and wide, especially in India, Russia, and Europe. Many festival and formal costumes were heavily adorned with buttons, which were used to create intricate patterns on fabric.

"Paste" or glass (costume) jewels became popular in England around the same time, and Birmingham in particular developed into a huge button-making center. Jewelers covered bone, wood, or horn buttons with elaborate metal designs or set them with stones. Buttons became family heirlooms and prized by collectors.

PEWTER PICTURE
BUTTON,
LATE 1800s

IVOROID STORY BUTTON,
LATE 1800s

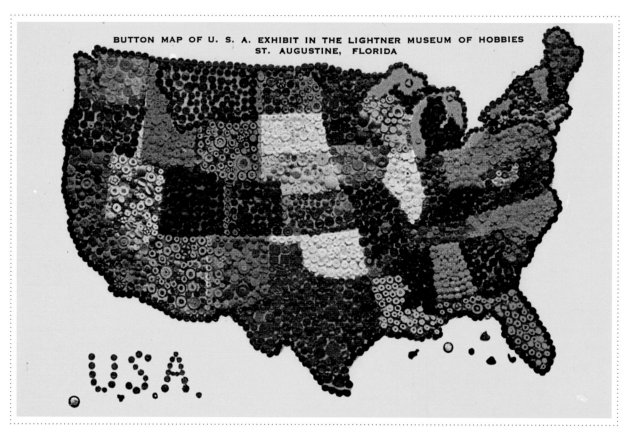

BUTTON MAP OF THE UNITED STATES

In early America, metalsmiths made buttons with copper or silver. Settlers traded buttons made from silver coins with American Indians, often used on coats or heavy shirts. In the late 1700s and 1800s, Pacific Northwest Indians began embellishing blankets and clothing with trade buttons. They created elaborate designs on simple wool blankets, often illustrating traditional motifs like a bird or animal with hundreds of small mother-of-pearl buttons. Decorative and ceremonial clothes also were made from blankets.

Meanwhile, politics and popular culture often influenced new button designs, such as those commemorating George Washington's inauguration or P.T. Barnum's introduction of circus elephant Jumbo, to name a couple of the most popular themes of their days. Flowers and all things botanical, fairy tales, children's stories, literature, animals, and architecture were other favorite themes.

SATSUMA STONE-
WARE BUTTON,
LATE **1800s**

ART DECO-THEMED BUTTON,
1930s

The Sewing Revolution

In the nineteenth century, button manufacturing increased rapidly in both the United States and Europe. The War of 1812 created a huge market for military buttons, and along with the invention of the sewing machine in 1845, it revolutionized garment and trim manufacture. Meanwhile, traveling salesmen brought buttons with them on new routes, opening distant markets up worldwide.

In the 1860s, young women in the United States collected buttons on a string—the first signature piece was especially elaborate (a "touch button") and the collections were carefully stored. The superstition was that when a woman's string numbered 999 or 1,000 buttons, her true love would appear. Another version says that upon a woman's engagement or marriage, her husband-to-be would add the thousandth (final) button to complete her charm string.

In England and throughout the British Empire, Queen Victoria's four-decade mourning period for her husband, Prince Albert, influenced button fashion. Jet and its cheaper and more readily available imitators, black glass and onyx, became the materials of choice, including embellishments.

A lightening of spirit and style arrived with Edward VII's reign at the turn of the century. Enameled and sterling silver buttons came to prominence during the Art Nouveau era of the late 1800s and early 1900s, including elaborately decorated pieces in motifs of the day (flowing, sinuous lines and stylized, feminine images). Asian designs became wildly popular in much of the West. Designers like René Jules Lalique and Carl Fabergé created lavish, romantic buttons, as well as the elaborate glasswork, jewelry, and their better-known art pieces.

The subsequent Arts and Crafts movement elevated handmade buttons and natural materials to greater prominence, signaling a shift in style. Buttons made after 1918 are considered "modern" and include many new materials and processes like casein and other plastic derivatives.

The 1920s brought a new way of dressing; the flapper era spotlighted fun-loving Art Deco styles, such as lavish Egyptian themes and exotic button materials like lapis, carnelian, and turquoise. Meanwhile, button mills and factories in the Northeast and Midwest did a booming business, spurred on by demand.

Button collecting again became popular in America during the Great Depression of the 1930s, when housewives began collecting and organizing

BAKELITE "COOKIE", 1930s

BAKELITE "REALISTIC" CLOTHESPIN, 1930s

Essex Pearl Button Factory, Arlington, N. J.

ESSEX PEARL BUTTON FACTORY IN ARLINGTON, N.J.

buttons as a hobby, rather than just saving them for reuse. Like brightly printed commercial feedsack fabrics, which were hugely popular for sewing, buttons became more colorful and less utilitarian, sparking a new enthusiasm for home sewing and remodeling older clothing, especially since money was tight for many people.

In the 1930s, glossy, gorgeous Bakelite also rose to prominence in the marketplace, though it later fell out of fashion due to its toxic ingredients and manufacturing process. Celluloid became popular as an alternative to ivory and other scarce materials. During World War II, plastic and wooden buttons dominated the civilian market since metal was scarce.

Mid-Century Arrivals

The 1940s and '50s brought the rise of "realistics," which were themed sets of fanciful mass-produced buttons shaped like tiny food, cars, animals, house-

COMMEMORATIVE
WORLD'S FAIR
BUTTON, 1939

VINTAGE CLOTHING
FABRIC BUTTON, 1950s

extraordinary
BUTTON SHOPS

Buttons can be found in a dizzying assortment of places—from mass-market fabric stores to eBay^SM and Etsy^SM. Two of my favorite smaller shops, one on each coast, have especially incredible selections.

exclusive buttons

In El Cerrito, Calif., Exclusive Buttons has been in the button business for more than 50 years. Vincent Sortile began selling buttons as a distributor to variety shops and, after eight years, he found himself more interested in the buttons than in his sales rounds. So he and his wife, Mary, opened a shop of their own, specializing in American-made buttons of the mid-century era, from the beautifully colored and detailed to the mass-market. They bought in bulk directly from manufacturers, ordering 5 to 50 gross of each design, and carded the array of buttons with their own logo. Their business thrived and home sewers, collectors, and enthusiasts have flocked to their shop.

The shop's inventory is huge, and their specialties include mirrored Czech crystal, hand-set rhinestone sparklers, and metal filigree, as well as the colorful casein and Bakelite that line the walls of the store. Some of the buttons in stock are rare and unusual pieces from 100 to 150 years ago, bought from private collections, but most of their inventory is the original, wonderful 1940s, '50s, and '60s buttons of all types and styles. Many are on their original cards and are in mint condition.

tender buttons

On the East Coast, button aficionados can shop at Tender Buttons in New York City. This tiny shop has a dazzling array of buttons, from sparkling crystal and Lucite, and colorful, charming sets of goofies to museum-quality antiques. Glance from one long, lined wall to the other to find intricate carved whalebone, delicate celluloid designs, dark Bakelite, and any other vintage material and style you can imagine. The presentation is immaculate and the shop itself is wonderfully inviting; don't miss the displays of truly incredible rarities, such as sets of early Colonial buttons and bejeweled European antiques.

Originally founded by Diana Epstein and Millicent Safro, who traveled the world acquiring collections and one-of-a-kind buttons, the shop has thrived since its opening in 1964. In their fantastic book, *Buttons,* they describe some of their most memorable buying trips, including sojourns to "a cave in Brussels, a Quonset hut outside of London, the head of a fjord in Finland, a souk in Cairo, a thrift stop in Moscow, and backstage at the Paris Opera." You can see the exquisite finds from around the globe framed neatly on cards and shown behind glass. For more on both shops, see Resources on page 166.

hold products, and all manner of iconic objects. Glittering costume jewelry–like designs rapidly changed with current fashion trends, and German and Czech-made glass was imported in record numbers. Buttons aligned more with modern pop culture than ever before, with designs rolled out to celebrate new Hollywood movies, world's fairs, hit records, and other exciting events of the day.

In the late 1950s and '60s, plastics and bright colors dominated, matching the eye-catching designs of the time: floral, abstract, geometric, and other striking patterns. Home sewing continued to be popular, and handmade dresses and clothes of the era often had charming, colorful buttons, including covered buttons with contrast or matching fabric.

Buttons from these decades abound on their original cards at flea markets and estate sales, and are relatively affordable compared to older, rarer specimens. Plastics, Lucite, and caseins are also very durable compared to some of the more fragile materials used in earlier eras.

The 1980s brought a resurgence in button production, with many new styles, including bright, graphic designs, Southwest-influenced and other fashion trends of the decade, and a corresponding rise in handmade buttons made of polymer clay and lampworked glass.

Today's buttons run the gamut from simple utilitarian rounds in whites and blacks to colorful, whimsical designs of all shapes and sizes that are available at large chain stores and tiny specialty shops. Many new mass-produced buttons are as fun to sew or craft with as the vintage pieces, and as a bonus, an enthusiast doesn't have to dip into her precious collection to make a project shine.

Styles

Many of these antique and vintage buttons fall into certain genres, depending on their theme, era, or visual reference. Here are some of the most prominent styles of buttons.

Stylized and decorated pieces like **ARCHITECTURAL, CAMPAIGN** (also known as political), and **LITHOGRAPHED** buttons show vivid, detailed scenes or images on a smooth or embellished surface (often round in shape).

"PICTURE BUTTONS" is a broad term including illustrative designs in carved or molded metal, or other materials, originally popular in Victorian times. **"STORY BUTTONS"** often reference a fairy tale, song, or poem.

Buttons reflecting current events or trends (military eras or Jenny Lind's visit to America, for example) are often called HISTORICAL. They are also referred to as SOUVENIR if they reference a specific event like a world's fair or advertise a product.

REALISTICS are tiny twentieth-century replicas of collectible or themed objects, such as toys, animals, or groceries, also known as goofies. They're usually made of plastic, though some are glass or other materials, and they're very collectible and prized by enthusiasts.

Materials

Here are some of the materials that made antique, vintage, and modern buttons. I've included some suggestions for identifying, cleaning, and caring for your collection. The books I recommend in the Resources section (page 166) have more information, too.

BAKELITE buttons, a form of plastic, became popular in the 1930s. They are often carved in detail and the colors are deep and rich—though they are never found in white or ivory colors, since the resin is naturally amber-colored. They are made in a chemically messy process and the toxic materials (carbolic acid, formaldehyde, and lye) and by-products are one reason they fell out of favor with manufacturers. Bakelite has a distinctive chemical smell when warmed in the hand. Wash pieces in cool or warm water (not hot) and dry well. Store them carefully so they don't deteriorate.

BONE buttons date back to the Stone Age, but more elaborately carved and decorated styles became popular in the 1850s and afterward. When magnified, they have an organic, porous look rather than completely smooth. Carved whalebone or teeth buttons are known as scrimshaw. Clean bone buttons with alcohol instead of water.

CERAMIC buttons represent by a wide range of eras and styles, from the simplest natural-colored clay to elaborate Wedgewood cameos. Porcelain pieces like Dresden or Delft were glazed or painted in much the same way as their fine china counterparts, and in the early twentieth century, it became fashionable for girls and women to paint their own buttons by hand. To clean ceramic buttons, wash them by hand as you would fine china. If you are unsure of the finish, be sure to clean an inconspicuous place like the underside first.

COVERED buttons can be embellished with beads or jewels or simply covered with a layer of fabric. Dorset buttons are neatly embroidered or knotted with embroidery thread for an elegant look, or woven in a spiderweb

WARTHER'S BUTTON MUSEUM, DOVER, OHIO

pattern. Embroidered buttons were often designed to match formal waistcoats or dresses. Buttons were also covered with a layer of crochet or knitting to match sweaters or coats. Depending on the material, they can be washed by hand or dry-cleaned.

ENAMEL buttons are kiln-fired so that a carefully arranged coating of ground glass over metal melts into a smooth, glossy, colorful surface. Variations like cloisonné were especially popular. Clean these with a damp cloth.

FROG or knotted buttons were first popular in China and are still used as fasteners today. Depending on the material, they can also be dry-cleaned or washed by hand.

GLASS buttons are one of the most popular materials—they were made famous in the era of Queen Victoria. Buttons were made in clear glass as well as translucent and opaque versions of every color, and typically have a metal shank. Glass buttons can be painted, enameled, or otherwise decorated, and many clear glass buttons are reverse-painted so that the detail or image is on the underside. One clue about how to identify glass is if a drop of water slides right off the button instead of beading up. Wash them by hand in warm, soapy water. Be sure to treat painted glass buttons with special care so as not to scrub off the decoration.

make your own
BUTTONS

Have you ever dreamed of creating your own buttons—either duplicating favorites from your own collection or using vintage molds? Here are instructions for doing your own casting, courtesy of Laura Stokes, a crafter and designer in Southern California, who hand-casts buttons and jewelry components for her line, Buzzard Brand. She says, "Like any new craft, it gets easier the more you do it. Being able to make your favorite buttons (and save money and time searching) is well worth it—the power of plastics lies in your hands."

Refer to buttonitupbook.com for Laura's complete instructions for creating an original mold using silicone, or try using vintage button molds, which can often be found on eBay.

You'll Need

Smooth-on resin *(resin and starter kits with color dyes and other additions are available at smoothon.com and dickblick.com)*

Mold (vintage or handmade)

Latex or nitrile gloves

Mask or respirator

Stir sticks (wooden popsicle sticks work well)

Plastic or paper cups

Paper towels

Trash bag

1. Find a sturdy flat surface to work on, like a desk or kitchen table. Cover it with newspaper to protect it, and be sure to wear a mask (or use a respirator) and gloves while you're working.

2. Prepare your mold. Pour your resin into equal parts in small plastic or paper cups—pour a small amount of part A into one and part B in another. If you want to add color, thoroughly mix it into cup B. Once that is well combined, add part A and mix thoroughly, and then pour it into your finished mold.

3. Keep in mind that you will not have very long to use your resin once part A and part B are mixed—some resins cure as soon as 10 minutes after contact, which means you will only have about a minute to stir and use it! Think fast and think ahead, and remember that if a button turns out differently than you hoped, you can always re-pour another one again afterward.

4. Once you pour your resin you will magically be able to watch it transform from a clear liquid to solid plastic in as little as 10 minutes. While the resin cures, clean up any surrounding mess with paper towels.

5. Pop your new buttons out of their molds and admire them!

· *For more about Buzzard Brand, see Resources on page 166* ·

HORN buttons came from a single piece of horn or from pressed, fused layers of horn, which lent itself well to elaborate designs. Horn usually has a gamey smell when it's warmed in the hand; wash them in cold water only, or gently wipe them with a soft cloth—you may want to use a small amount of furniture polish to shine them. TORTOISESHELL was a specific kind of horn in shades of brown, amber, and yellow. Today this generic term refers to any plastic or other material of the same appearance.

IVORY buttons were traditionally made of elephants' tusks, though hippopotamus or walrus tusks were often used. Ivory was often carved elaborately or painted, and frequently found as an inlay material in a metal button frame. Clean ivory with alcohol instead of water, and treat it carefully, since it grows more brittle with age.

JET is made from coal and is relatively unusual and difficult to find. It is lighter in weight than glass or onyx. Most "jet" buttons found today are black glass. Real jet will smell faintly of coal when warmed; clean it with alcohol.

LEATHER buttons are typically a toggle or shank style instead of drilled. Clean them by wiping them with a soft cloth and leather polish.

METAL buttons are historically among the most popular worldwide. Elaborate gold or sterling silver buttons were made for royalty in the Renaissance. In the early 1800s, metal buttons began to be mass-produced in Birmingham, England (the jewelry manufacturing center of Britain), and were relatively inexpensive. Brass is the single most popular material (typically used for uniforms), though aluminum and other alloys are also common.

Many shank-style metal buttons have designs, motifs, or decorative scenes on the front. Metal buttons can be lacquered, painted, engraved, etched, cloisonnéd, enameled (covered with fused glass), or set with glass or stone cabochons. Gently polish and clean metal buttons with a soft brush or cloth; do not overpolish them or you can damage the surface.

PLASTIC first appeared in England in 1862 and became popular in the United States a decade later, when John Wesley Hyatt pioneered celluloid. Casein, which uses milk protein, is another early version, as is Lucite (an acrylic). Originally, plastic was made to simulate amber or ivory, and then became popular in its own right. Plastic buttons come in a huge range of styles and colors; most are opaque and can be custom-dyed to match fabric or thread. Wash them in cool or warm water (not hot) and dry well. Clean celluloid with a damp cloth.

SEMIPRECIOUS buttons were popular during the Victorian era and afterward, particularly agate, carnelian, coral, and jade. Amethyst and amber are rarer. They are found in both faceted and cabochon (smooth) flat-backed versions with shanks, as well as inlaid in metal or other materials. Clean them carefully and do not soak them in water.

Some of the most popular versions of SHELL buttons are mother-of-pearl and abalone, which are often carved into cameos or other shapes. Freshwater pearl buttons were made from the 1890s onward from shells found in the Mississippi River. These buttons were stamped out and drilled in local factories. Meanwhile, ocean pearl buttons were made in Japan and the Philippines in a thriving industry, until the fighting in the Pacific during World War II put an end to button production. When factory production finally resumed after the war ended, the price of pearl buttons rose significantly. Ocean shell buttons are typically used for utilitarian purposes. Hand-wash antique pieces without soap or just gently rub them with a towel; modern shell buttons, such as those on garments, are usually machine-washable.

VEGETABLE IVORY buttons are made from the corozo nut of the Tagua palm tree, a South American plant. The material can be dyed or embellished with great detail, and generally ages well. It substitutes well for ivory, which has become scarce. To clean them, wipe gently with a soft cloth, but don't use water.

WOOD buttons first appeared in the 1700s and became more elaborate in the next century. They became very popular during World War II. Hand-wash wood buttons and dry them immediately. If you use any wood polish, take care not to get it on other button components (like metal frames).

Types of Buttons

There are two main types of buttons: shank and sew-through.

SHANK buttons have a small loop or drilled post on the back for an elevated setting.

SEW-THROUGH buttons are drilled, usually with two or four holes, and are sewn on flat.

Look for a back mark showing the manufacturer's or artist's name or symbol on antique and older vintage buttons. This was the practice for hundreds of years, but in mass-produced plastic, casein, and Bakelite buttons, the manufacturer's name is more often on the card the buttons originated on rather than each individual piece.

2

TECHNIQUES & MATERIALS

Whether you're a beginner or a more experienced crafter, here are some suggestions for what you'll need to get started—including materials, tools, and techniques.

I've organized everything into jewelry-making, sewing, and gluing sections for convenience, so you can just flip to the ones you need as you plan your project.

jewelry 101

Making jewelry with buttons is fun and very open-ended—with few basic tools and materials on hand you can create just about anything that comes to mind.

First, you'll need a set of three **PLIERS**:

- **FLAT-NOSE PLIERS** (also called chain-nose pliers) are ideal for flattening or forming sharp angles.
- **ROUND-NOSE PLIERS** are for forming smooth loops and curves. Their jaws graduate in size so you can make tiny loops around the narrow tips or larger loops farther back on the wider sections.
- **WIRE CUTTERS** are for neatly clipping wires and cords.

For knotting between buttons or to add bead tips, you can use long, skinny-tipped **TWEEZERS** to grip the cord right where you want your knot to go.

Then there are the materials you'll use to create jewelry projects, from stringing components to the findings that finish off your piece.

WIRE comes in different gauges or thicknesses—the higher the gauge number, the thinner the wire. For many projects, **20- AND 24-GAUGE WIRE** is perfect. Thinner or thicker wire may be called for too, but these are ideal to start with.

CRAFT WIRE is inexpensive and generally a bit softer and more pliable than precious metal wire; it's made of base metal, which is an alloy, or mixture, of different materials. Use it for practicing or for higher-volume projects like the Button Curve necklace on page 56.

STERLING SILVER AND GOLD-FILLED WIRE are both wonderful to work with. They come in different levels of hardness—I like **HALF-HARD** wire, which has more strength and body than **DEAD SOFT** wire, which is more pliable.

JUMP RINGS are useful for joining two pieces together, like chains to clasps. A jump ring is just a circle of wire that isn't sealed shut—it can be opened with pliers and then closed again. They come in a range of sizes.

EYEPINS are straight pieces of wire with a small loop at the end.

EARRING WIRES, which range from simple drops and hooks to more elaborate leverbacks, come in post styles as well. **CLASPS** come in many forms, too, from plain to ornate—S-shapes, lobster claws, barrels, and toggles, to name just a few.

Add buttons to blank **HAIRPINS**, **BRACELETS**, **RINGS**, and **MAGNETS** for pretty, personalized projects. Vintage and new **METAL CHARMS** and elements are fun to work with. Add a **PINBACK** to a button or embellished metal piece to create an instant brooch.

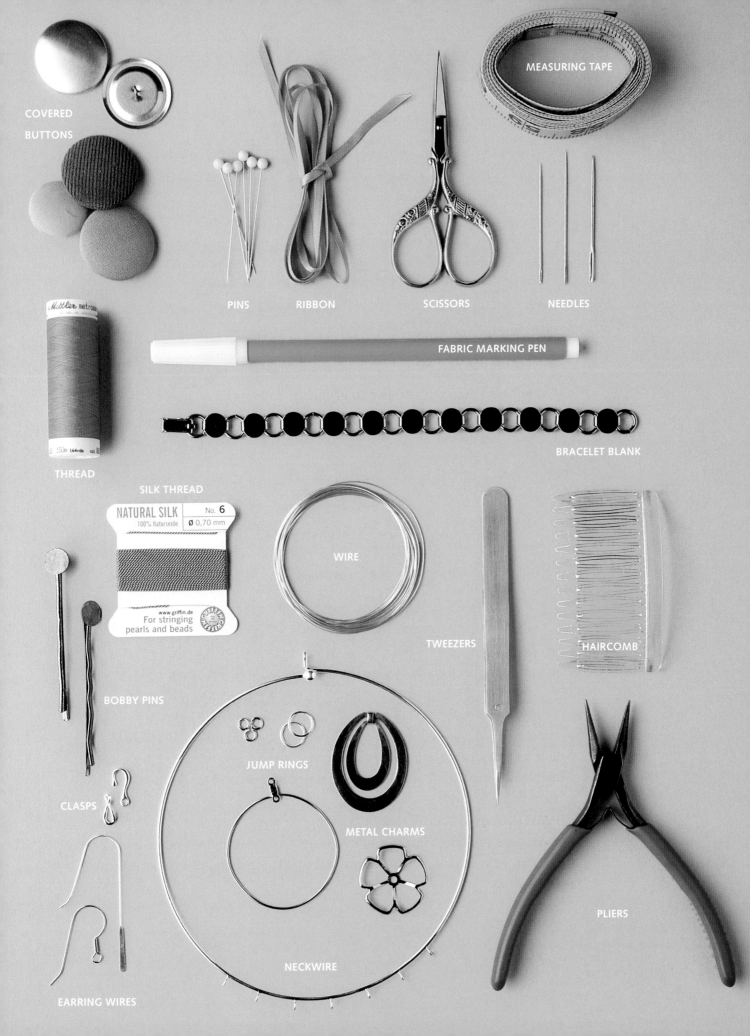

COVERED
BUTTONS

PINS

RIBBON

SCISSORS

NEEDLES

MEASURING TAPE

FABRIC MARKING PEN

THREAD

BRACELET BLANK

SILK THREAD

NATURAL SILK
100% Naturseide
No. 6
Ø 0,70 mm

www.griffin.de
For stringing
pearls and beads

WIRE

TWEEZERS

HAIRCOMB

BOBBY PINS

CLASPS

JUMP RINGS

METAL CHARMS

PLIERS

EARRING WIRES

NECKWIRE

FLEXIBLE BEADING WIRE (such as Soft Flex®) is a coated wire that's durable, supple, and great for heavier beads or pendants.

Use small cylindrical **CRIMP BEADS** to finish the ends of your flexible wire or ribbon pieces—I highly recommend sterling silver or gold-filled crimp beads instead of base metal. **BEAD TIPS** are perfect for ending a knotted or strung piece.

BEADING NEEDLES can be used with thin cords of all types. **SILK** or **NYLON BEADING CORD** in various thicknesses is perfect for knotting between buttons. Many silk cords come on a card with a twisted wire needle, which is especially easy to use.

Narrow **RIBBONS** can be lovely to use—it can be easier to slip a crimp bead on at the end of a strand if you cut the ribbon at a diagonal so it has a point much like a needle. If it frays after you've beaded with it, just trim it to a point again.

CHAIN comes in all kinds of styles and materials. Choose an open circle or link chain for bold pieces, or thin, delicate chain for smaller-scale work.

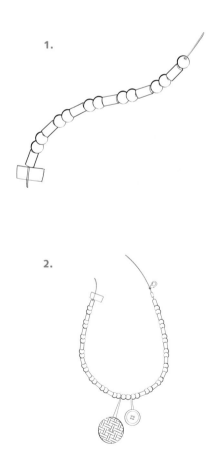

1.

2.

JEWELRY TECHNIQUES

FLEXIBLE BEADING WIRE

You don't need to use a needle to string beads with flexible wire, making it an easy way to create a necklace or bracelet. Seal the ends with crimp beads for a durable, sleek finish.

1. Cut a piece of wire at least 4 inches to 6 inches longer than the finished length of the piece you're making. Add a doubled piece of clear tape near the end of your wire to hold your design as you string your piece—it's easy to take off when you're ready to finish the ends but won't kink or untie itself as a knot often does.

2. Begin creating your design from one end, or construct the middle section and move outward—it's up to you. Beads will slip right onto your wire, so you don't need a needle. Just add them in the desired pattern and, remember, you can always tape the working end and switch back to the other side if you want to change your design—it's very flexible.

3. If you need to take a break or don't finish the project right away, just tape both ends of the wire to hold the pattern.

CRIMP BEADS

1. Finish stringing your piece of jewelry. Place a single crimp bead on the end of the strand and add a clasp. Slip the wire tail back through the crimp bead and then through the next several beads on the strand.
2. Tug the wire so it's taut, with no gaps between beads or at the end.
3. Firmly flatten the crimp bead closed with your flat-nose pliers.
4. Clip off the end of the wire close to the beads so the end tucks back in—otherwise they can scratch your skin.

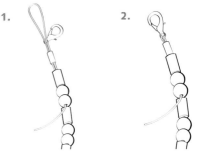

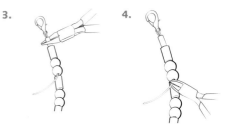

KNOTTING

Knotting between buttons or inside a bead tip is easy—especially when you use narrow tweezers to pinpoint exactly where you want your knot to go.

1. Choose where you want your knot to be, and grip that spot firmly with tweezers.
2. Bring your working cord around and over to tie a simple square knot over the tip of the tweezers.
3. Move the tweezers away just as you tighten the knot closed.

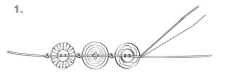

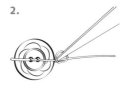

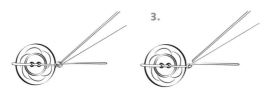

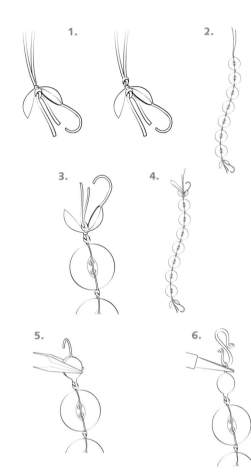

BEAD TIPS

Bead tips work well with silk and other cords. The tips cover a knot at each end of the cord securely, and the curved hook attaches to clasps or other findings.

1. Tie a knot near the beginning of your cord and slip one bead tip onto it, with the two cupping halves facing and enveloping the knot (as shown at left). Knot again directly above the bead tip to keep it in place.
2. String or knot your beads as you go until you're happy with your piece. Tie a knot at the end of the bead strand.
3. Add a bead tip with the halves facing outward, away from the beads and toward the needle. Using your knotting tweezers to pinpoint the spot, tie a knot inside the tip and pull it taut.
4. Add a drop of Fray Check® or glue (I often use Fray Check first and then, after it dries, glue) and snip the cord ends away just above each knot.
5. Using flat-nose pliers, press the tips closed around the knots.
6. Using round-nose pliers, curve the hook around a jump ring or clasp loop.

BUTTON WEAVING

Make a knotted necklace or bracelet by weaving two cords through the holes of sew-through buttons. If you use four-hole buttons, simply pass the cords through two of the holes diagonally.

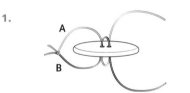

1. Begin with a knot (see "Knotting" on page 23) and then separate your two cords—think of them as A and B.
2. Weave A through your first button—from front to back and then through the second hole back to front.
3. Weave B in the same direction, but starting from the opposite side—back to front, then front to back. This catches your button neatly between the two strands.
4. Adjust the button so that it is very near your first knot and both ends are even.
5. Now knot again on the other side of the button to hold it in place.
6. Repeat all the way around the piece, ending with a knot and another bead tip.

WRAPPED LOOP

This coiling technique creates a durable loop at the end of a strand of wire.

1. Cut a piece of wire, or grasp the wire tail of a project in progress about two or three in from the end, with your round-nose pliers, and make a neat 90° angle bend.

2. Adjust the round-nose pliers so they are gripping on either side of the wire bend, above and below it. Use your flat-nose pliers to pull the wire tail over the end of the round-nose pliers and all the way around, creating a circle with an extra tail of wire still extending beyond it.

3. If you are joining the loop to a chain or clasp, slip it into the open loop now.

4. Use the flat-nose pliers to hold the circle while you grip the end of the wire tail with your round-nose pliers. Slowly wrap the wire tail around, working from top to bottom to create a neat coil.

5. Clip the end of the wire flush with the coil, making sure the sharp edge isn't sticking out—if it does, use your flat-nose pliers to flatten and smooth it into the coil.

1.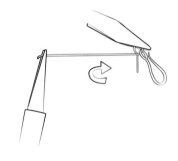

2.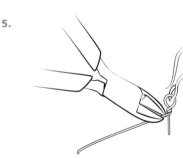

3.

4. **5.**

1.

2.

3.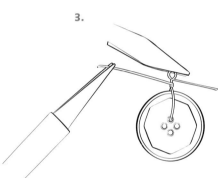

4.

5.

BUTTON DANGLES

This dual loop wraps around and through a sew-through button to connect it to your chain or cord, forming a double connector or hanger. It's essentially two wrapped loops, one above and one below, that meet in the middle.

1. Cut a piece of wire and form a bend about ⅓ of the way from one end. Slip the wire through the top hole in a sew-through button, with the longer end in front, shorter one behind.

2. Use the same coiling technique from the Wrapped Loop on page 25 to coil the shorter (back) wire around the longer (front) one, keeping the long one straight. Wrap the wire two or three times.

3. Form a second loop above the coil. If you are joining it to a chain or another loop, slip it onto the other component now while the loop is still open.

4. Complete the wrap by coiling downward until you meet the first coil, making sure the wire ends are tucked to the back of the coil so they don't show.

5. Clip both wire tails and neatly flatten them to the back if they are rough.

> **TIP:** As you wind the top wrap in step 4, the coil will stay neater if you bring the wire around on the opposite side from the first wrap, as shown.

WIRE LOOPING

This technique is great for wiring sew-through or shank buttons to a larger piece, like the Red and Gold Wreath (see page 158) and Pretty Pencil Cup (see page 154) projects.

1. Cut a long piece of wire and form a wrapped loop at one end.
2. Thread the working end of the wire through or around your object. Bring it back around to form a loop around the whole piece.
3. Thread the end of the wire through the wrapped loop circle and pull it taut to hold it. This has the same effect as tying a knot when sewing—it keeps your first "stitch" in place.
4. Continue wrapping the piece or adding buttons—slip the wire through the first hole in a sew-through button, back to front, and then through the second hole, front to back—or through a shank from side to side.
5. Continue embellishing your piece the same way. If you run out of wire or it snaps, just wrap it toward the back and start again at step 1 with a new piece of wire.
6. Finish by twisting the wire together at the back of your piece. You may want to secure the twist with a drop of glue.

1. INSIDE

2.

JUMP RINGS

Use jump rings—small circles of wire with an opening—to attach clasps, suspend charms, or form a simple chain.

1. Open a jump ring by gripping the ring on each side of its opening with a pair of pliers. Separate the ring by tilting the right side toward you and the left side away from you— don't pull the ring open into a U shape, but use a twisting motion so it doesn't misshapen.
2. Close the ring by reversing step 1. The ring should close neatly with no gap where the ends meet. If it doesn't meet neatly on the first try, gently tilt the two sides back and forth past the closed position a few times until the ring "clicks" shut. You can also make sure it's secure by squeezing it shut with the flat-nose pliers.

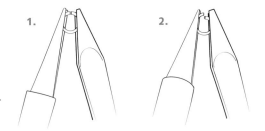

1.   2.

TIP: To attach a clasp to a chain, simply slip both the last link in the chain and the clasp (or its ring) onto the open jump ring in step 1. Close it to connect the two, as in step 2.

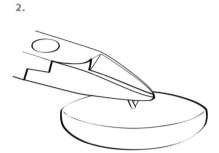

1.

2.

3.

When you need a flat back for your embellishment or jewelry project, you can cut the loop right off a shank-style button with wire cutters or special shank clippers. This method, recommended only for new or inexpensive buttons, is ideal for plastic and lighter metal, glass, or wood buttons. Be very careful with glass and heavier metal shanks; though they may not come off as easily or at all, so definitely wear eye protection when trying to clip them.

1. Turn your button over so that the shank is facing up. Grip the entire shank or one side if it is thicker, with your wire clippers and gently but firmly squeeze the handles. If it does not cut immediately, stop and adjust the angle slightly, then try again.

2. If you are only cutting one half at a time, shift to the other side and cut that one carefully, too.

3. If there are rough edges left on the back of the button, gently clip them away with the wire cutter or try light- or medium-grit sandpaper to smooth them down.

Sewing 101

A handful of basic tools and materials are all you need to get started sewing and crafting with buttons.

Sharp SCISSORS are a must—I like to tie a ribbon through the handle of a small pair and wear them around my neck so they're always right at hand.

Embroidery or hand-sewing NEEDLES come in a range of sizes—having a good collection on hand makes things easy. If you are stitching buttons onto fabric or another form for embellishment, I suggest using POLYESTER sewing thread (not cotton), which is more durable over time. EMBROIDERY FLOSS comes in a wide array of colors and creates a gorgeous line for embellishments. And an EMBROIDERY HOOP is ideal for working neatly and precisely on a taut surface. A washable FABRIC MARKING PEN is perfect for drawing a design on fabric—a few drops of water make any lines disappear. And a MEASURING TAPE is ultra-handy for all your sewing and embellishment projects.

When you're choosing fabric, keep in mind that medium-weight cotton is nice for pillow covers, while a heavier wool, cotton, corduroy or twill is ideal for bags or pieces that are more durable. Wool or acrylic felt is perfect for toys or other small projects—it doesn't fray so it's easy to use without hemming.

SEWING TECHNIQUES

SEWING ON A BUTTON
To stitch a button onto fabric, follow these simple instructions.

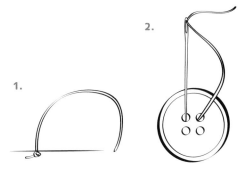

SEW-THROUGH:
1. Thread a needle and tie a knot at the end of the thread. Bring it through your fabric back to front at the spot you'd like your button to sit.
2. Bring the needle up through one hole and down through the next one, bringing it back to the underside of the fabric. If you are sewing on a four-hole button, stitch it on in two parallel straight lines instead of back and forth diagonally (unless you want to create an "X" effect).
3. Continue sewing in the same channels several times to reinforce your stitches.
4. Tie another knot behind the button on the underside of the fabric to secure it, and clip your thread.

. . . .

SHANK:
1. Thread a needle and tie a knot at the end of the thread. Bring it through your fabric back to front at the spot you'd like your button to sit.
2. Bring the needle through the shank, in one side and out the other, continuing down through the fabric to the underside again.
3. Repeat several times to reinforce your stitches and then knot your thread securely on the underside of your fabric.

> **NOTE:** If you're sewing a button on a garment or functional piece to use with a buttonhole or other fastener, you may want to add an extra "shank" of thread behind it for lift.

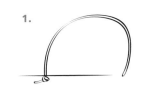

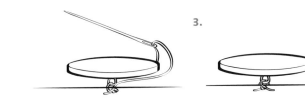

RUNNING STITCH

This simple forward stitch is the easiest way to join two pieces of fabric with thread or make a decorative broken-line design.

1. Thread a needle and knot your thread. Bring it up from the back (wrong side) of your fabric through to the front so the knot is on the underside.

2. Stitch ahead, moving your needle forward as shown at left, following the pattern of your choice—straight, curved, or angled. You can easily vary the length or distance between your stitches to change the look of them.

BACKSTITCH

This method is a bit more involved, but it creates a more durable join since it is reinforced by doubling back with each stitch. The stitches on the front of your fabric will look as neat as a running stitch, while the back will have overlapping longer stitches showing.

1. Thread a needle and knot your thread. Bring it up from the back (wrong side) of your fabric through to the front so the knot is on the underside.

2. Bring your needle back into the fabric *behind* where it emerged as shown at left. You'll double back instead of stitching forward. To begin the second one, bring the needle well out in front of the completed first stitch, then double back again the same way. You can also vary the length or placement of your stitches as with the running stitch, but it works best for a straight line rather than any curve or elaborate pattern.

COVERED BUTTONS

Cover plain shank-style buttons with fabric for a super-personalized project. You can find vintage or new covered button kits to use—just snap the two halves together with the fabric of your choice. Here are two methods for creating your own customized covered buttons, depending on which style of kit or materials you have.

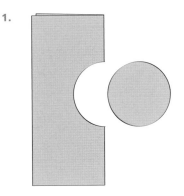

MOLD METHOD

1. Using the template on your package, cut out a circle of fabric.
2. Press the fabric, right side down, into the small mold. Now press the button front into the mold so that the fabric edges are sticking out evenly all the way around.
3. Arrange the fabric edges inside the button hollow so that they're totally concealed. Now press the button back into the mold, reinforcing it with the pusher until it snaps into place.
4. Pull your finished button out—it's ready to use.

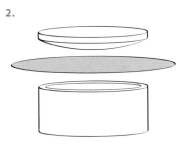

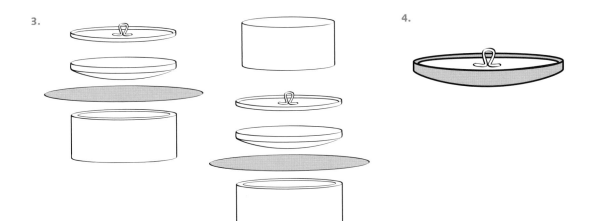

1.

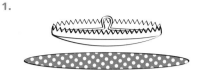

2.

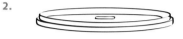

3.

COVERED BUTTONS CONTINUED
TEETH METHOD

For this version, you'll stretch your fabric over the button front and catch it in sharp little "teeth" instead of using a mold. Once the fabric is smoothed over the front of the button, press the button back over the raw edges of the fabric, using a spool of thread for extra weight if necessary.

> **TIP:** For a sheer fabric, using two layers makes a nicer-looking button. For stiff or heavy fabric, dampening it makes it easier to handle.
>
> And if you're using a patterned fabric and want to spotlight a particular part of the print on your button, the teeth method makes it easier to pinpoint your front design, rather than the mold, which hides the working fabric until it's set.

MACHINE SEWING

Several projects in the book give the option of MACHINE SEWING (though you can always hand-sew or add your own touches to a premade piece instead of starting from scratch). If you're not that familiar with machine sewing, I recommend some fantastic books for reference, including:

READER'S DIGEST COMPLETE GUIDE TO SEWING

BEND-THE-RULES SEWING by Amy Karol

SIMPLE SEWING by Lotta Jansdotter

SEW SUBVERSIVE by Melissa Rannels, Melissa Alvarado, and Hope Meng

Gluing 101

You'll also use glue in some projects, especially to embellish. Here are my suggestions and recommendations, depending on what you're working with.

CRAFT GLUE (recommended brand: Aleene's® Tacky Glue®) is ideal for attaching small lightweight pieces to flat surfaces and will not damage the color or backing of a rhinestone.

CEMENT GLUE (recommended brand: Bond 527) is perfect for adding an embellishment layer to a button or metal piece. I'd also suggest Aleene's Glass and Bead glue for mirrors or other shiny/resistant surfaces.

FABRIC GLUE (recommended brands: Aleene's OK To Wash It or Fabric Fusion® for heavier pieces) is machine-washable or dry-cleanable, so it's ideal for attaching buttons to a garment or other fabric project.

SILICONE GLUE (recommended brand: DAP®) is a good general glue that works well with magnets or other heavier pieces.

HOT GLUE GUNS are great for joining larger or varied pieces to a base, such as the Row of Sparkles haircomb project on page 139.

INDUSTRIAL-STRENGTH GLUE (recommended brand: E-6000®) is the strongest bond of all, but make sure you have plenty of ventilation when you're gluing with it. Two-part epoxy is also good for creating a strong join.

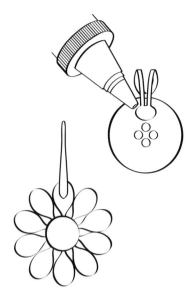

GLUING TECHNIQUES

GLUING A BUTTON TO A SMALL SURFACE

To add a button to a component like a paddle-style loop, ring or bracelet blank, or chain link, use a small- to medium-size dab of strong, clear-drying glue such as cement glue or industrial glue. Apply the glue to the metal finding and then press the button into it, unless the finding is especially small (like a pendant bail) in which case it's easier to put the glue on the button and then press the piece into it that way. For a magnet, I recommend silicone glue, which has a thicker consistency. Use a generous amount of it to hold the magnet in place.

GLUING A BUTTON TO A LARGER SURFACE

To glue a button to glass or fabric, you'll typically use a more generous dose of glue as well. For gluing to fabric, make sure to saturate the surface under the button so that it adheres well, and let it dry completely before moving it. For gluing to glass or mirrors, you can use hot glue—again, a bigger dab is ideal—and press the button directly into the glue, or use a similar technique with cement or glass and bead glue.

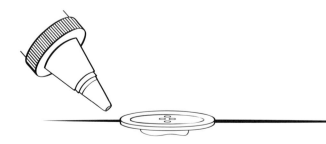

How to Use This Book

Button It Up includes a range of jewelry, sewing, and crafts to try your hand at making. So if you want to find out how easy or advanced a sewing project is or how long that pair of earrings will take you from start to finish, there are a set of icons for each project in the book. Look for them at the beginning of each project set.

E = easy

M = moderately hard

A = an advanced project

= takes less than an hour to make

= sew-through buttons only

= shank-style buttons only

I've also listed all the techniques you'll need to use to make a project, boxed like this:

Techniques

PLAIN LOOP *(PROJECT NAME)*
WRAPPED LOOP *(PROJECT NAME)*
JUMP RINGS *(PROJECT NAME)*

Tips

are quick suggestions on other materials to use, a shortcut, or ideas to change the size or fit of the piece.

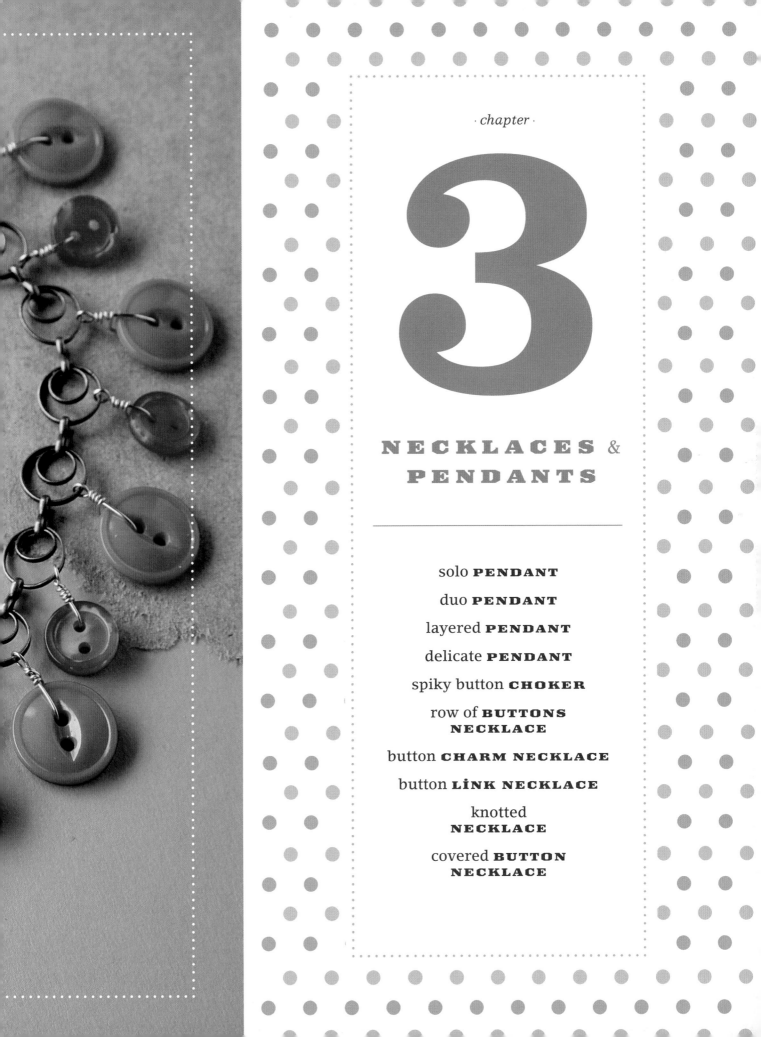

· chapter ·

3

NECKLACES & PENDANTS

solo **PENDANT**

duo **PENDANT**

layered **PENDANT**

delicate **PENDANT**

spiky button **CHOKER**

row of **BUTTONS NECKLACE**

button **CHARM NECKLACE**

button **LINK NECKLACE**

knotted **NECKLACE**

covered **BUTTON NECKLACE**

solo
PENDANT

Choose a striking button for this stand-alone design. For example, a medium-size piece will hang nicely from a delicate chain, while a bolder shank style will dominate a sleek neckwire.

Techniques

GLUING,
JUMP RINGS *(VINTAGE FLOWER)*

VINTAGE FLOWER

You'll Need

Pliers

Cement glue

Button

Pendant bail

15½ inches of delicate/medium chain

Two jump rings

Clasp

1. Glue the pendant bail to the top of the back of the button, aligning the holes as you want them to appear when the pendant hangs down. Let it dry completely.

2. Slip the pendant onto the chain. Use jump rings to attach one half of a clasp to each end.

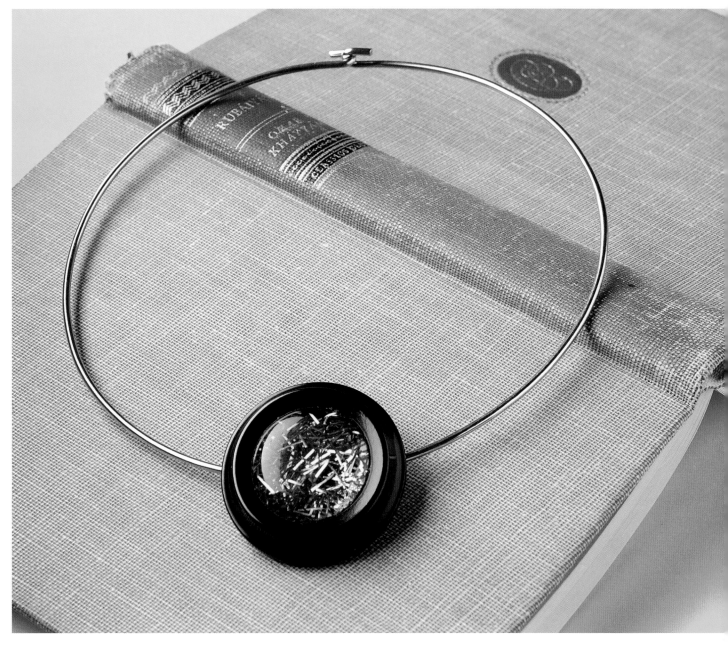

You'll Need

Large or medium button (with shank large enough to slip over neckwire)

Neckwire

Industrial-strength glue (optional)

SPARKLE POP

Slip the button onto one end of the neckwire and let it slide to the center. If desired, fix it into place with glue and let it dry completely. (If you don't glue it, the button will stay facing forward as you wear it, but may move around the neckwire.)

duo
PENDANT

This arrangement of a smaller button suspended above a larger one is quite versatile. Use two sizes of the same design or two very different buttons in a style or color family. Of course, a very random pairing works, too.

DUAL LINES

You'll Need

Pliers

Cement glue

Two similar or identical buttons in different sizes

Three flat silver oval findings

Two jump rings

Neckwire

1. Turn the buttons face down and arrange the flat ovals on the backs so that the smaller button has one end overlapping at the top and bottom, and the larger one has one overlapping at the top.

2. Use cement glue to attach the findings to the buttons. Let it dry completely.

3. Attach the two buttons with a jump ring. Add a jump ring to the top button loop and slip it over the neckwire before closing it.

LINKED UP

You'll Need

Pliers

Two buttons (I used a smaller sew-through and a larger filigree shank style, but you could use two of either type)

Three oversized jump rings

One small jump ring

16 inches of ribbon

1. Open the three larger jump rings and slip them through the two holes in the upper button, and through the filigree space (or hole) in the lower button. Close each jump ring.

2. Open a smaller jump ring and use it to link the two buttons via the larger jump rings.

3. Slip the top (unlinked) jump ring onto your ribbon.

layered
PENDANT

Techniques

BUTTON DANGLE *(COLORED VINYL)*,
GLUING

Juxtapose two buttons in different sizes and colors together for a simple, striking pendant design. Whether you join them with wire or glue, the larger piece framing the smaller one can create a very interesting effect.

You'll Need

Pliers

20-gauge wire

Two sew-through buttons, one larger than the other

Chain of your choice

Industrial-strength glue

COLORED VINYL

1. Stack your two sew-through buttons together, smaller on top of larger, so that the holes are aligned.

2. Cut 6 inches of wire and form a curving bend about 2 inches from one end. Thread the long end of the wire through one button hole and the short end through the other, front to back, and tug the wires through so that the curve is the only part that shows on the front.

3. Twist the shorter piece around the longer one two or three times to join them and clip the end neatly. Gently bend and press the twisted wire tails so they are flattened together and vertically aligned up the back of the larger button. The longer strand will stick straight up above the buttons when you look at them from the front.

4. Now you'll make a button dangle above the button's top rim with the longer strand. Form a front-facing loop and coil beneath it to meet the top of the button, as shown in the photo, and clip the end neatly.

5. Press the wire spine against the back of the button pendant again so that it hugs the back of the piece. Glue it down with industrial-strength glue and let it dry completely before wearing it.

6. Slip the pendant onto the chain.

You'll Need

Industrial-strength or cement glue

Two buttons of your choice, one larger than the other (either sew-through or with the shanks clipped off)

Pendant bail

Chain of your choice

CIRCLES AND CURVES

1. Arrange your buttons together with the smaller one off center. When you like the placement, apply glue to the back of the smaller button and carefully press it into place. Let it dry completely.

2. Turn the layered buttons over and add a small dab of glue on the back, right at the top of the button. Press the pendant bail down and let it dry completely.

3. Slip the pendant onto the chain.

delicate
PENDANT

These designs use a streamlined metal piece rescued from a broken piece of costume jewelry to spotlight a single, central button.

Techniques
GLUING,
CRIMP BEADS *(BUTTON BLOSSOM PENDANT),*
JUMP RINGS *(BOTH),*
BUTTON DANGLE *(MOD DELUXE)*

Tips
You can adapt the basic Mod Deluxe idea to use whatever vintage or new jewelry bits and pieces you have on hand—try pairing a button with a similarly shaped or sized metal "frame."

You'll Need

Cement glue

Pliers

Scissors

Shank or sew-through button

Metal filigree-style or open flower

Jump ring

20 inches to 24 inches of ⅛-inch-wide ribbon

Two large crimp beads

Clasp

BUTTON BLOSSOM PENDANT

1. Glue the button to the center of the flower and let it dry completely. Open the jump ring and attach it to one petal at the top of your pendant piece, closing it securely.

2. Trim your ribbon's ends at a sharp diagonal angle, so you will be able to thread them through the crimp beads more easily. Slip the pendant ring onto the ribbon and center it. Slip one crimp bead onto each end of the ribbon, pushing them down 3 inches or 4 inches.

3. Add the clasp to one side, and then double the ribbon back through the crimp bead, catching the clasp in the loop of ribbon. Make sure that the ribbon isn't twisted and that it's lying flat.

4. Repeat step 3 to add the ring to the other side. Make sure that your pendant ribbon is the right length and make any adjustments you'd like.

5. Use flat-nose pliers to crimp both beads securely, then trim the excess ribbon tails with your scissors.

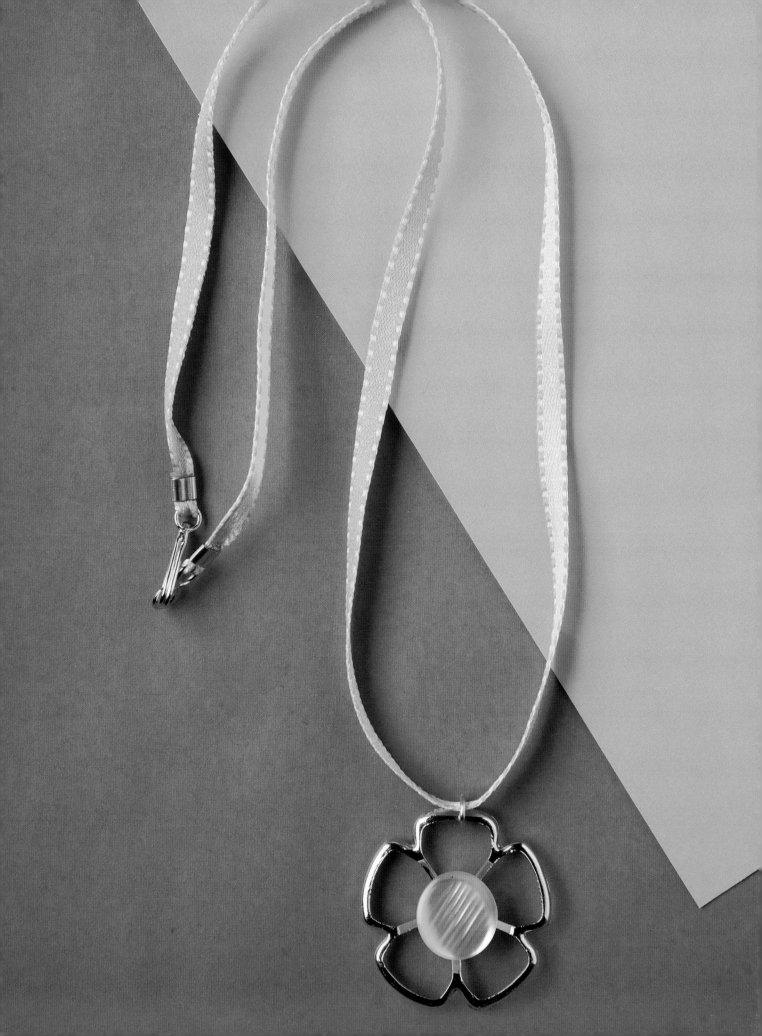

You'll Need

Pliers

Cement glue (optional)

24-gauge wire

Button of your choice

Open metal oval or circle that mimics the button's shape, drilled or with a ring at the top

Two jump rings

Chain of your choice

MOD DELUXE

1. Form a button dangle using 24-gauge wire. If you'd like to secure the wire on a larger button, add a small dab of glue to the back of the button so it stays in place.

2. Use a jump ring to join the button dangle so it hangs within the metal frame piece and, if necessary, add a second jump ring above so it can hang on the chain.

3. Slip the chain through the jump ring and close it securely.

spiky button
CHOKER

Techniques

GLUING,
JUMP RINGS *(BRIGHT BLUE DROPS),*
BEADSTRINGING *(WOOD DUAL DROPS)*

A grouping of buttons suspended on spare, extended paddle-style spikes really emphasizes the style of each one. Whether you arrange a larger number of identical buttons across the center or isolate two mismatched pieces together, the effect is striking and very easy to wear.

E

You'll Need

Pliers

Cement or industrial-strength glue

Seven small buttons

Seven paddle-style drops of varying lengths (I used one 1¼ inch long in the center, with two 1¹/₁₀-inch, two 1-inch, and two ¾-inch paddles radiating out from the longest one.)

Seven small jump rings

Neck wire with loops

BRIGHT BLUE DROPS

1. Turn all seven buttons face down and use a dab of cement or industrial glue to attach a paddle drop to each one. Let them dry completely.

2. Open seven jump rings and use them to attach the button drops to the neckwire loops, arranging the drops in order of length.

You'll Need

Pliers

Cement or industrial-strength glue

Tape

Two wood buttons (I used one that was 1¾ inches across and one that was 1 inch)

Two wood paddle-style drops (mine were 2 inches and 1 inch long)

Wood beads, round and cylinder styles

20 inches of Soft Flex wire

Two crimp beads

Clasp and ring

WOOD DUAL DROPS

1. Attach the buttons to the paddle drops the same way as the Bright Blue Drops version and let them dry completely.

2. Place the larger drop on the beading wire and add two round beads on each side. Add the smaller drop to the right and add two more round beads on the right side of the paddle.

3. Continuing to work in the same direction, add one cylinder bead and two rounds, repeating this pattern for 6½ inches. Secure the open end with tape.

4. Repeat step 3 on the other side of the necklace to extend the same pattern for 7 inches. Your necklace should now have the larger drop in the center with the smaller one just off to the right.

5. Attach the clasp to one end using crimp beads and attach the ring to the other the same way. Clip the ends of the wire.

row of BUTTONS NECKLACE

This project spotlights an odd number of buttons in a simple but eye-catching formation. Try arranging them symmetrically and spaced evenly for an especially pleasing effect.

For the Buttons and Beads version, the seed beads you choose for this necklace need to be small enough to easily pass through the holes in your buttons. Size 15 seed beads should work well. The instructions given are for a standard 16-inch choker-sized necklace where the buttons lie nice and flat against your neck. You'll want to measure your neck to determine the perfect choker size for you.

Techniques

**WIRE-WRAPPING,
JUMP RINGS** *(BUTTON CURVE),*
BEAD STRINGING *(BUTTONS AND BEADS)*

Tips

Using different buttons in the same color family is a nice way to spotlight favorites that don't quite match in the Button Curve design.

You'll Need

Pliers

....

One package of seed beads that are size 15 or smaller

....

Beading needle and 25 inches of thin beading thread (for a standard 16-inch choker necklace)

....

Nine sew-through buttons

....

Two jump rings

....

Clasp

BUTTONS AND BEADS

1. Thread your beading needle, string eight seed beads in a row, and go back through the very first bead you threaded. Then go through the other seven beads you threaded. This forms a loop of seed beads where you'll eventually attach one end of the clasp.

2. String about 4 inches of seed beads and then pass the needle through one hole of a button. String about five more seed beads and pass the needle through the opposite hole of that button. Now you've strung the seed beads through the button and the button should be nicely held in place by the beads.

3. String seed beads for about 2 more inches and repeat step 2.

4. Repeat steps 2 and 3 until you have a necklace that's 16 inches long or the length you'd like.

5. Finish off the other end of the necklace with a seed bead loop as instructed in step 1. Tie a square knot at the end of the loop and snip the thread.

6. Now attach the clasp pieces to the seed bead loops. Using the flat-nose pliers, attach one jump ring to each loop. Attach the clasp to one of the jump rings.

· By Leah Kramer ·

You'll Need

Pliers

24-gauge craft wire

5 vintage buttons of your choice

Delicate or medium-weight chain

Two small jump rings

Clasp

ALTERNATE VERSION
with three buttons

For this one you'll make your necklace the same way, but use a slightly shorter piece of wire and longer pieces of chain (for a 17-inch necklace I used two 6½-inch lengths of chain). In step 1, slip 3 buttons on the wire instead of 5, and follow the directions accordingly.

BUTTON CURVE

1. Cut a 30-inch piece of craft wire and slip the five buttons onto it one by one, facing forward and in the order you prefer, so that they're evenly spaced about ¼ inch to ½ inch apart, and the last one is about four inches from one end.

2. Cut two pieces of chain, each 5½ inches long. Make a forward-facing plain loop with your short wire tail, ½ inch from the last button. Slip the last link of one length of chain onto the wire and into the loop. Wrap the working wire tail around the button-row wire neatly to form a coil, and clip it after two or three wraps, making sure the end is tucked to the back.

3. Form a plain loop the same way ½ inch from the button on the other end, with a very long wire tail extending outward. Slip the other piece of chain into this loop as in step 2 (or close it and use a jump ring to attach them later).

4. Gripping the loop with your flat-nose pliers, begin coiling the wire tail around the wire frame the same way as step 2, but continue wrapping instead of cutting it off early. Wrap it neatly until you reach the first button, then bring the working wire straight across the back of it and continue coiling between the first and second button.

5. Continue across the entire necklace frame until you reach the short coil on the other end. Wrap right up to it, until your working wire is flush with the coil then clip it neatly, tucking it to the back.

6. Use jump rings to attach the clasp and ring to each end of the open chains. If your necklace is too short or too long, remove the clasp and adjust the length now.

button CHARM NECKLACE

Techniques
BUTTON DANGLES, JUMP RINGS

Tips
Use a lobster or hook clasp to keep this necklace adjustable, and add an extra button (or two) to the other end of the chain to embellish the design.

This necklace pairs a series of dangling buttons with a pretty open-link chain for a traditional charm bracelet effect. Design yours with a repeating pattern all the way around or a centered arrangement to suit your style.

You'll Need

Pliers

16½ inches of circle chain

Gold 24-gauge wire

12 medium-size buttons

11 small buttons

One jump ring

Lobster clasp

RED DASHES AND DOTS

1. Working left to right, use a jump ring to attach the clasp to the left end of the chain. Set one small and one medium button aside, and create dangles with the other 21 buttons, leaving the top loop open.

2. Attach a medium button dangle 1½ inch in from the left end of the chain, closing the top loop. Then attach a small button dangle to the next link.

3. Alternating between medium and small buttons, attach the next 19 dangles so that you have 21 of them arrayed across the necklace, with extra space left on the far (right) end of the chain.

4. Create a button dangle with the remaining medium button and close the top loop. Make a second button dangle through the small button, linking it to the medium dangle before you close the loop.

5. Then create a dangle through the other hole in the small button, linking it to the last link of the chain.

You'll Need

Pliers

16 inches of silver filigree chain

Silver 24-gauge wire

One large button for the center

Seven medium buttons (can be identical or assorted; I used two of one kind and five of another)

Hook clasp

SUNNY DAYS

1. Use a jump ring to attach the clasp to the left end of the chain. Create dangles with all of the buttons, leaving the top loop open, and setting one medium button aside.

2. Working left to right, measure 5 inches in and add a medium button dangle to a link of chain.

3. Add two more medium dangles, spacing them evenly (I added mine to the smaller round links in the chain pattern, about an inch apart).

4. Add the large button dangle and then three more medium dangles, all spaced the same way as in step 3.

5. Attach the last medium dangle (the one you set aside in step 1) to the right end of the chain as an embellishment.

button
LINK
NECKLACE

Link buttons you especially like into a chain pattern for this necklace design. You can use a combination of over-sized and smaller jump rings to join your buttons, or link the buttons themselves with eye pins.

Technique

JUMP RINGS *(CIRCLES AND BLOSSOMS)*

Tips

If you are using jump rings to connect your button links, save time by opening them all at once before you start the project.

You'll Need

Pliers

Seven medium-size buttons (I used three of one style and four of another, in the same shade of blue)

Eight open plastic circles

Large jump rings

Small oval jump rings

Clasp and ring

CIRCLES AND BLOSSOMS

1. Open the large jump rings and slip one into a button hole. Close it with your pliers. Repeat until all seven buttons have closed jump rings through both holes.

2. Repeat step 1 with the eight circles, so each one has two closed jump rings on it.

3. You'll connect each of these buttons and circles using smaller oval rings. Join them one at a time, beginning with a circle and alternating circle-button-circle, and so on. If you are using more than one button style, you can alternate those, too.

4. When your chain of buttons and circles is complete, it should lie flat with all buttons facing up. If any are backward, just open the small jump rings and flip the button over so it lies facing up.

5. Use small jump rings to attach the clasp and ring to the necklace ends.

You'll Need

Pliers

Three large flower buttons (about the size of a half-dollar coin)

Two smaller buttons (about the size of a dime)

One clasp (any style you like!)

Two 1-inch eyepins

Four 1½-inch eyepins

10-inch to 14-inch chain of your choice

VINTAGE FLOWERS

1. To get started, place all the buttons face down in the desired order.

2. Working from left to right, slide one of the 1½-inch eyepins through the hole of one of the larger buttons and then through the hole of one of the smaller buttons to connect them, wrapping the end securely around the shank of the smaller button. Slide a 1½-inch eyepin through the second large button and then again through the first small button and wrap the end securely around the shank of the smaller button. You should now have three buttons attached in this order: large, small, and large. Two 1½-inch eyepins are through the hole of the small button (one coming from the left, one from the right).

3. To finish the centerpiece, you'll repeat step 2. Slide a 1½-inch eyepin through the hole of the second large button and then through the hole of the second small button. Wrap the end securely around the shank of the smaller button. Slide a 1½-inch eyepin through the hole of the third (and final) large button and through the hole of the second small button. Wrap the end securely around the shank of the smaller button. You now have five buttons attached in this pattern: large, small, large, small, and large.

4. Cut two pieces of chain, each 5 inches to 7 inches long. This can be adjusted depending on how long or short you'd like the necklace.

5. Slide a 1-inch eyepin through the first and third large buttons going in the opposite direction from the eyepin that is already there. Attach the chain on either side with the 1-inch eyepin.

6. Attach the clasp to the left side chain. Now you have a vintage button link necklace!

· By Christy Petterson ·

knotted
NECKLACE

This design suspends a neat array of buttons woven on silk or nylon cords, with knots between each one. Mix assorted buttons in the same color family together or create a sleek, sophisticated version with identical shimmering shell buttons.

Techniques

BEAD TIPS, WEAVING, KNOTTING

Tips

Use a cord with enough body to slip through the buttonholes without a needle, but make sure it's thin enough to pass easily through each one twice.

If you are using an assortment of buttons, arrange them so some of your favorites are near the center and will be more visible.

You'll Need

Pliers

Knotting tweezers

Cement glue

Scissors

Assorted buttons in the same color family (I used 23 to make my necklace)

6 feet of nylon beading cord, cut into two 3-foot pieces

Two bead tips

Clasp and ring

S H I R A Z

1. Tie a secure knot about 3 inches from one end of cords #1 and #2, knotting them together. Add a bead tip and secure it with a knot on the other side (you may need to use double knots if your cord is thin and the bead tip passes over the first knot).

2. Slip your first button onto cord #1, weaving it though the holes. Now weave cord #2 through the holes from the opposite side to secure the button with the two cords holding it in place.

3. Use your tweezers to make a knot just past the first button.

4. Repeat steps 2 and 3 to add as many buttons as desired, weaving and knotting each one the same way.

5. When you've added your last button, make a secure knot or double knot just after it. Add a bead tip to this end the same way as in step 1.

6. Snip the excess cord off at both ends and add a drop of glue to secure each knot inside its bead tip. Close each bead tip cup and let the glue dry completely.

7. Add the clasp and ring to the ends of the necklace and close the bead tip hooks to secure them.

You'll Need

Pliers

Knotting tweezers

Cement glue

Scissors

Mother-of-pearl or shell buttons (I used 17 to make my necklace)

6 feet of white nylon beading cord, cut into two 3-foot pieces

Two bead tips

Clasp and ring

PEARLESCENT

Make this version of the necklace the same way as the Shiraz necklace (see page 66) using identical white mother-of-pearl buttons. The process is essentially the same, but the effect is quieter and more traditional, like a strand of perfectly matched pearls.

covered
BUTTON
NECKLACE

Techniques

**COVERED BUTTONS,
GLUING** *(TRIPLE DIP FEED SACK NECKLACE)*

Using covered buttons to design a necklace gives you a completely new way to customize your piece, depending on the fabric you go with. Designer Cathy Callahan chose textured burlap to work with, while Jennifer Perkins of Naughty Secretary Club says, "Feed sack is the perfect fabric to use when covering buttons. Due to the small pattern and colorful print you can get a lot to look at on just one button."

You'll Need

Scissors

....

Covered buttons (I used two ¾-inch, four 1-inch, and six 1¼-inch buttons)

....

Fabric (I used three colors of burlap)

....

2 feet of 2mm leather cord—other options are ribbon or hemp. (Choose something around this thickness or bigger so that your buttons will stay in place while strung on it.)

BURLAP BUTTONS NECKLACE

1. Decide on color, fabric, and sequence of buttons for your necklace. I used a repeating sequence of colors and arranged smaller buttons on the sides and larger ones at the center.

2. Cut fabric for the buttons, cover them, and snap the backs on.

3. String the buttons on the cord in the order you like. Tie the cord in a bow instead of using a clasp.

· By Cathy Callahan ·

You'll Need

Craft glue (recommended: Aleene's Liquid Fusion)

Pliers

Three oval discs drilled on either side

Eight jump rings

Clasp

Three 1⅛-inch covered buttons

Fabric with small and colorful print, like feedsack

Plastic binding spiral links (or chain of your choice)

TRIPLE DIP FEEDSACK NECKLACE

1. Choose your fabric and cover three buttons. (They don't have to match if you are that kind of gal.)

2. Use your pliers to remove the shanks from the back of the buttons and glue your buttons in the center of three flat discs. (I used some yellow plastic ovals that I had on hand, but feel free to use what you have.)

3. Connect your spirals to form a chain. (I used green spiral links to contrast nicely with the yellow ovals.) These links, which are from the teacher store, are like split rings so they link easily to make your chain as long or short as your little heart desires.

4. After your glue has dried, use your pliers and jump rings to attach the three oval discs to each other, with a spiral link between each one. Attach equal lengths of the plastic chain to the two outside oval discs.

5. Add a jump ring to one side and a jump ring plus lobster clasp to the other.

· By Jennifer Perkins ·

button
POST
EARRINGS

This is an easy and surprisingly sophisticated way to turn just two (or four, or six) buttons into gorgeous post earrings.

You'll Need

Industrial-strength glue

Two buttons

Two post-style earring blanks

RED ROUNDS

Set the buttons facedown and apply a dab of glue to each back. Press the earring posts into each one and let dry completely.

You'll Need

Industrial-strength glue

Two large sew-through buttons

Two medium dome-shaped sew-through buttons

Two small shank buttons that fit inside the dome buttons

Two post-style earring blanks

VINTAGE COSTUME

1. Set the large buttons face up.

2. Apply glue to the rounded top of the dome-shaped buttons and press one onto the center of each large button. It should look like you have a bowl sitting on a plate.

3. Apply a generous amount of glue to the shank of the small buttons and press one into the center of each inverted dome button. Make sure you use enough glue to hold the shank buttons upright. You may need to hold them for a minute or two until the glue sets.

4. Once the glue has dried, place your button stacks face down. Apply a dab of glue to each earring post and press one into the back of each large button, close to the edge that you would like to be the top of the earring.

5. Let dry completely.

· By Torie Nguyen ·

button
DROP
EARRINGS

Choose two bold shank-style buttons for this simple but elegant design. They look fantastic suspended drop-style on paddle wires.

PRETTY IN PINK

You'll Need

Cement or industrial-strength glue
....
Two shank-style buttons
....
Two paddle-style earring wires

1. Slip one button onto each earring wire and let it settle on the paddle—it should be suspended just above the bottom of the drop.

2. If desired, add a drop of glue to secure it. Gravity should keep it in place if you don't glue it, though it may move around a bit.

SILVER SPOTLIGHT

You'll Need

Cement or industrial-strength glue

Pliers

Two metal shank-style buttons

Two paddle-style drops (mine measured 1¼ inches)

Two small jump rings

Two leverback earring wires

1. Attach the paddle drops to the back of each button with a dab of glue and let dry completely.

2. Use a jump ring to attach each drop to a leverback earring wire.

button
DANGLE
EARRINGS

These spare earrings swing low for an effect that's somehow more than the sum of its (very simple) parts. The feminine floral shapes lend an unexpectedly pretty sense to an otherwise uncluttered design.

Technique

BUTTON DANGLES *(LONG AND LOW FLOWERS)*

Tips

If your buttons for the Filigree Flowers earring design aren't actually filigree, simply create a button dangle (as I did for the Long and Low Flowers earrings) and slip that onto your elongated earring wire instead of threading it through a space in the button's pattern.

LONG AND
LOW FLOWERS

You'll Need

Pliers

Two flower-shaped buttons

24-gauge silver wire

Chain-style earring wires

1. Use your 24-gauge wire to create button dangles with each button, leaving the top loop open.

2. Slip the top loops into each earring wire ring and close the loops.

FILIGREE FLOWERS

You'll Need

Two filigree-style buttons

....

Two elongated earring wires

1. Slip a filigree button onto the earring wire, back to front, so that it comes to rest in the dip at the front of the wire.

2. Repeat with the second button and earring wire.

button
HOOP
EARRINGS

Techniques

WRAPPED LOOP,
WIRE LOOPING *(AUTUMN LEAVES)*

Spotlight a handful of your favorite buttons on a front-facing circle! Create a repeating pattern all the way around, or simply arrange a mix of sizes on a wire hoop.

You'll Need

Pliers

Cement glue

24-gauge craft wire

Two flat circle hoops for embellishing (mine were 2 inches across)

12 small buttons

10 wooden beads

Four vintage metal leaves

Two headpins, if drilling circle at the top

Earring wires

AUTUMN LEAVES

1. Cut two 2-foot pieces of craft wire. Form a wrapped loop at one end and loop your wire around the top of the circle hoop, threading the tail through the wrapped loop and catching it so it's concealed at the back of the piece.

2. Working left to right, wrap the wire closely three times around the front of the hoop. Then slip your first button onto the wire tail and wrap it securely onto the circle so it sits in place. If the circle were a clock face, the button would be in the one o'clock spot.

3. Wrap the wire three more times and then slip a wooden bead onto the wire tail so it sits in the two o'clock spot.

4. Continue adding alternate buttons and beads, with three wraps between each one, around the circle. At the seven o'clock spot, add two metal leaf charms, one on each of those in-between wire loops. Continue the pattern after the leaves the same way, ending with a final button just before the 12 o'clock spot. If you run out of wire or your wire breaks, just tuck it toward the back and secure it with a drop of glue, and start again with a new piece of wire as in step 1.

5. Finish by tightly wrapping your wire tail around after the final button, and clip the excess wire away. Secure your last wrap by pressing it with your pliers and then adding a drop of glue.

6. Make your second earring the same way, but place the leaf charms from step 4 at the five o'clock spot for symmetry on this one.

7. If your circle has a loop at the top, slip each one into the earring wire. If it's drilled, slip a headpin through each hole at the top and loop the headpin around to form a simple circle there. Slip that through the earring wire.

You'll Need

Pliers

Two front-facing metal hoop circles

Assorted buttons in the same color family (I used 18 blue buttons in a variety of sizes)

Post-style earring wires with loops

BLUE ARRAY

1. Arrange your buttons into two sets, each an odd number (I used nine per earring). I organized mine so that the smallest were on the edges and the larger ones were in the center. You can make a stack of buttons or spread them out one by one.

2. Open each hoop circle at one side. Slip the buttons on in order so that they hang down on the hoop in the arrangement you chose in step 1.

3. Close the hoop circles back up. Open the earring wires' loops and slip the circles onto them so that they face forward. Close them securely.

button
L I N K
B R A C E L E T

Glue a set of sew-through buttons onto a blank
bracelet or a section of flat chain for a simple,
pretty bracelet

Techniques

GLUING

 JUMP RINGS *(AMBER SQUARES)*

Tips

*Choose a bracelet blank or circle chain with
large enough flat spaces to support your
buttons—use smaller, lighter buttons for a
more delicate style, and larger buttons for a
sturdier version.*

PINK ROUNDS
LINK BRACELET

You'll Need

Cement glue

....

Blank link bracelet

....

Six medium-size assorted
buttons

Glue one button into each bracelet link and let
dry completely.

AMBER SQUARES
LINK BRACELET

You'll Need

Pliers

Cement glue

Six large brown square buttons

7 inches of circle chain with flat connectors

Two small jump rings

Magnetic clasp

1. Lay the chain out flat and set one square button on each second connector, leaving space at each end and between each button so the bracelet can move freely.

2. When you are pleased with the placement, attach each button with cement glue and let dry completely.

3. Use jump rings to attach the magnetic clasp to each end.

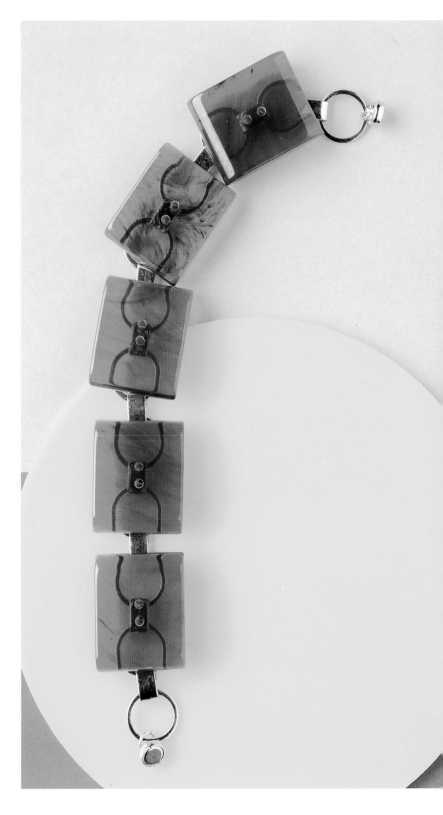

button
CHARM
BRACELET

Create a charm bracelet spotlighting your favorite vintage buttons! Whether you use an alternating arrangement or an exuberantly random mix, this is a fun way to show off a handful of buttons you especially like.

Techniques

BUTTON DANGLES, JUMP RINGS

Tips

If you're using assorted buttons, be sure to balance the weight of them across the bracelet so it doesn't hang unevenly or pull down in one spot when you wear it.

You'll Need

Pliers

....

Six large buttons

....

Five small buttons

....

24-gauge gold wire

....

7 inches of circle chain

....

Two small jump rings

....

Clasp

GLOSSY REDS AND PINKS

1. Working left to right, use a jump ring to attach the clasp to the left end of the chain. Create dangles with all 11 buttons, leaving the top loop open.

2. Attach a large button dangle one link in from the left end of the chain, closing the top loop. Then attach a small button dangle to the next link.

3. Alternating between large and small buttons, attach the next nine dangles so that you have 11 of them arrayed across the bracelet.

4. Now use jump rings to attach the magnetic clasp halves to each end of the chain.

You'll Need

Pliers

12 assorted silver-colored buttons

24-gauge silver wire

7 inches of plain link chain

Two small jump rings

Clasp

You'll make this bracelet the same way as Glossy Reds and Pinks (see page 91), substituting 12 assorted silver buttons and 7 inches of plain link chain. Arrange the buttons randomly so that no two identical ones are next to one another.

button CUFFS

These cuffs are fun to wear—and a nice departure from the sparkly side of things. Cover a close-fitting wristband with dozens of buttons, or quilt a stylish linen wraparound cuff with clean lines and contrast stitching.

BUTTON-COVERED BAND

E | ⏱ | ⊞

You'll Need

Sewing needle and thread

Scissors

Close-fitting wristband

Assorted small, medium, and large buttons in a similar color (I used 48 to cover my cuff)

1. Thread your needle and choose the center of your cuff. Pair a large plain button with an interesting smaller one and stitch them on like a watch face—this will be the focal point of your cuff design.

2. Add more large and medium-size buttons, overlapping them slightly as you go around the cuff. Fill in the gaps and spaces with smaller ones.

BUTTONY FABRIC CUFF

You'll Need

Scissors

Needle and thread

Sewing machine (recommended)

Straight pins

Iron

Fabric marking pen

Linen, fabric of your choice for the back, and quilt batting—each cut to 9 inches by 3 inches

Four to six buttons

3 inches of elastic

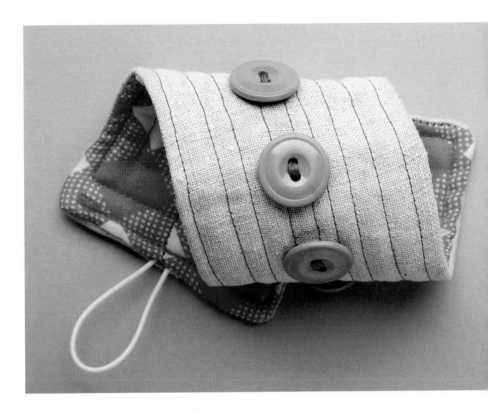

1. Layer the three fabrics in this order: batting, lining fabric, and linen (wrong sides facing). Pin them in place.

2. Beginning on a short side, stitch around the piece, leaving a 1½-inch opening on that first short side. Trim the edges and clip the corners.

3. Turn the cuff right side out through the opening and press it flat.

4. Loop the elastic cord and tuck the raw edges well inside the opening, and pin the open space closed.

5. Quilt the cuff in the pattern of your choosing (I used a contrast color thread), starting at the open end and stitching that securely.

6. Arrange the buttons in a row on the cuff, being sure to place one in a position to catch the elastic loop as a clasp. Mark the spots and stitch them in place with embroidery floss or thread.

· By Amanda Blake Soule ·

knotted
BUTTON
BRACELET

This bracelet style is a secure way to showcase a neat row of buttons around the wrist. Make one to match your knotted necklace or grab a handful of favorites for this piece. Try using a contrast or complementary beading cord, depending on your preference.

Techniques

BEAD TIPS, GLUING, KNOTTING, WEAVING

You'll Need

Pliers

Cement glue

Scissors

Eight wooden buttons

Wine-red beading cord, two 2-foot pieces

Two bead tips

Clasp

WOODEN ROUNDS

1. Tie a secure knot about 3 inches from one end of the cords, knotting them together and creating a stopper. Add a bead tip and secure it with a knot on the other side (you will need to use a double knot if your cord is thin and the bead tip can pass over the knot).

2. Slip your first button onto cord #1, weaving it though the holes. Weave cord #2 through the holes from the opposite side so that the button is secured with the two cords holding it in place.

3. Use your tweezers to make a knot just past the first button.

4. Repeat steps 2 and 3 to add all eight buttons the same way, weaving and knotting each one the same way.

5. When you've added your last button, make a secure double knot just after it. Add a bead tip to this end the same way as in step 1.

6. Snip the excess cord off at both ends and add a drop of glue to secure each seed-bead knot inside its bead tip. Close each bead tip cup and let the glue dry completely.

7. Add the clasp and ring to the ends of the bracelet and close the bead tip hooks to secure them.

You'll Need

Pliers

Cement glue

Scissors

Seven assorted blue and green buttons (about the size of a quarter)

Blue beading cord, two 2-foot pieces

Two bead tips

Clasp

UNDER THE SEA

Make this bracelet the same way as the Wooden Rounds version (see page 96).

layered
BUTTON
BRACELET

Pairing two buttons to make neatly layered bracelet links is a fun way to mix colors and styles.

Techniques

BUTTON DANGLE *(RED AND GOLD)*,
HAND-SEWING, GLUING *(SPRINGTIME MIX)*

Tips

Depending on the size of your buttons, or the number of links on your bracelet blank, you may need to adjust the number of buttons you use for this design.

SPRINGTIME MIX

You'll Need

Needle and thread
....
Scissors
....
Industrial-strength glue
....
Six medium-size buttons (I used pink)
....
Six small buttons
....
Bracelet blank with six links

1. Stack each set of the two buttons together to form pairs and make sure that the larger ones peek out below the top layer for contrast.

2. Use your needle and thread to stitch the first pair together, catching the knot underneath the larger button. Sew through the holes two or three times to secure them and conceal the knot underneath the stack.

3. Repeat step 2 to join the other button pairs.

4. Apply glue to each bracelet link and press each button pair onto a link. Let it dry completely.

RED AND GOLD

You'll Need

Pliers

Six smaller buttons (I used metal rounds)

Six larger buttons to "frame" them (I used red casein)

24-gauge wire

Clasp and ring

1. Stack each set of the two buttons together to form pairs and make sure that the larger ones peek out below the top layer for contrast.

2. Turn your first button pair into a button dangle, being sure to include both buttons in the wire loop so they hold together.

3. Now create a button dangle through the other holes, so that the button pair has become a bracelet link with loops on both sides.

4. Repeat steps 2 and 3 with your next button pair, but before you close the loop on the second button dangle, slip the open loop into one of the loops on the first one to join it to your first link.

5. Continue creating bracelet links until you have six joined together, but don't close the loops on the two outer ends yet.

6. Slip your clasp and ring onto the ends of the bracelet, and complete the wraps to finish the piece.

button
RINGS

Show off pretty, sparkly buttons or layer a shiny rhinestone over a plain one for an eye-catching cocktail-style ring that takes just minutes to put together. This is a perfect instant-gratification craft project to wear to a party or give as a gift.

Technique
GLUING

Tips
Always use industrial-strength glue to join the button to the ring blank, but be sure to use cement glue directly under a rhinestone; the industrial glue can eat away at the finish, dimming the sparkle.

CENTER SPARKLE

You'll Need

Cement glue

Industrial-strength glue

Sew-through button of your choice

Rhinestone that's smaller than your button

Ring blank

1. Use cement glue to attach the rhinestone to the top of the button. Let it dry completely.

2. Use industrial-strength glue to attach the button layer to the flat top of the ring blank.

> **ALTERNATE VERSION**
>
> To make a similar ring with a single sparkly button, just clip the shank off the back and apply a generous dab of glue to the back of the button. Press the ring blank into it and let it dry completely.

GLAM COCKTAIL

You'll Need

Wire cutters

Industrial strength glue

Two or more buttons, one
smaller than the other

Ring blank

1. Lay out your design and see how the buttons
   stack together. If there are any shanks that don't
   allow the buttons to lie flat, use the wire cutters
   to take them off.

2. Glue the buttons to one another.

3. Once completely dry, lay the button piece on a
   flat service and glue the ring base to the button
   piece. Make sure the piece is secure and unable
   to shift during drying.

· By Christina Loff ·

button
BROOCH

Spotlight a favorite button in the center of a brooch—
whether it's a hand-painted porcelain antique or sparkly
rhinestone, the layered framing effect brings it to life.

Techniques

GLUING (*RED BIRD*),
HAND-SEWING (*VINTAGE SPARKLE*)

RED BIRD

You'll Need

Industrial-strength glue

**Shank-style button of your
choice for center button**

**Larger sew-through button of
your choice for backing button**

Pinback

1. Layer your buttons together as you like and
   apply a generous dab of glue to the center
   of your backing button. Press the shank of
   the center button directly into it and let it dry
   completely.

2. Turn the brooch over and glue your pinback to
   the center of the back, about ¼ of the way down
   from the top edge. Let dry completely.

VINTAGE SPARKLE

You'll Need

Needle and thread

Scissors

Pinking shears

Cement glue (optional)

Two or more vintage buttons in various sizes—one shank-style for center, and sew-through for the others

Small piece of wool felt

Pinback

1. Arrange your buttons in an order you like. Once you have your button combo ready, stitch your buttons together to hold in place, knotting your final stitch. Set aside.

2. Cut out a small circle or square piece of felt that is slightly larger than your back button. Use pinking shears to make it extra fancy. Stack buttons on top of felt and sew the layers together until your button stack is secure. Knot in the back of the felt.

3. Sew your brooch to your pinback. Loop over as often as you need to make it secure. If you do not like the way the pinback and stitches look, you can cut a tiny piece of felt, the same size as the pinback, and affix it over your stitching with a dab or two of glue.

· By Jessica Wilson ·

· *chapter* ·

5

HOUSEWARES

button **MAGNETS**

vintage button
CAFE CURTAINS

button **KITCHEN SET**

flowered **TABLE SET**

dinner **PARTY SET**

button **BATH SET**

embellished button **PILLOWS**

button **DECOR**

button
MAGNETS

These magnet sets are super easy to whip up—all you need is a handful of buttons, glue, a stack of magnets, and fifteen minutes. Add metal flower frames for a pretty touch.

Technique

GLUING

Tips

If your buttons are light in color, you may want to apply a quick coat of white acrylic paint over the dark magnets and let them dry completely before gluing.

Order magnets in larger quantities to save money, instead of buying them in small packages at the craft store.

(E) (clock)

You'll Need

Silicone glue

Cement glue (optional)

Buttons

Magnets (one per button)

Small buttons, rhinestones, or other embellishments (optional)

GRAB BAG

1. Place your magnets on a horizontal magnetic metal surface, like a tray, spacing them at least an inch or two apart. Apply a dab of silicone glue to the top of each one and press a button onto each of them. Let them dry completely.

2. If desired, add a rhinestone or a smaller button to some or all of your button magnets for embellishment, using cement glue—it's up to you!

(E) (clock)

You'll Need

Silicone glue

Cement glue

Buttons

Metal flowers

Magnets (one per button)

DAISY MAGNETS

To make these magnets, just glue a button to the center of a metal flower, using cement glue, and let it dry. Then glue the flower to a magnet with a dab of silicone glue.

vintage button CAFE CURTAINS

This is a fun sewing project—cafe curtains whipped up from a set of tea towels or cloth-napkins. They're quick to make since all the edging is already done for you. You could also try using vintage or new scarves (filmy ones would be nice) or cut a patterned pillowcase in half and hem the side edges.

Techniques

HAND SEWING,
MACHINE SEWING *(RECOMMENDED)*
(CHEERFUL FLOWERS),
GLUING *(LOOP-D-LOOPS)*

Tips

Use buttons to embellish or enhance any existing pattern on your tea towels or fabric.

You'll Need

Iron (recommended)

Sewing machine (recommended)

Needle and thread

Measuring tape

Pins

Two matching or similar tea towels (mine measured 26 inches long by 20 inches wide)

Assorted vintage buttons (I used about 50 for mine)

Tension curtain rod to fit your window

CHEERFUL FLOWERS

1. Fold the short end of each tea towel down to form a channel for the curtain rod (mine worked well at 1½ inches; it slipped over the ends of the rod but wasn't loose). Iron or smooth it down and pin it in place. This will be the top of your curtains.

2. Stitch each seam by hand or with a machine. Test it to make sure it fits over the tension rod, and rip it out and re-sew it if it's too big or too small.

3. Now it's time for the fun part: arranging and sewing on the vintage buttons! Hand-sew each button on, bringing the needle and thread through three times to hold the button in place.

4. I added one button to the center of each flower, and used lots of different styles and sizes in orange, red, green, and yellow. It could also look great with a repeating print and identical buttons . . . or a simpler style with a button here and there as an accent. I threaded four needles, each with a different color, and just picked up a new one every time I added a different color button, but you could use the same thread each time if you like for simplicity.

5. When you have finished adding as many buttons as you want, slip the curtains onto the tension rod and place it where you'd like it in the window. This is perfect for a cafe-style curtain, with window peeking out above or below, rather than a measured or fitted style.

You'll Need

Fabric glue

Fabric marking pen

Measuring tape

Two cloth napkins (mine measured 20 inches square)

Assorted sew-through buttons (I used about 120 for mine)

Curtain clips

Tension rod to fit your window

LOOP-D-LOOPS

1. Lay out the first napkin flat on a piece of newspaper or scrap paper and mark the horizontal center. This will be the center of your middle loop-d-loop. Draw a simple pattern with the marking pen as a guideline for placing your buttons—it should be symmetrical, side to side.

2. Place buttons all along the loops with a tiny space between each one. Make any adjustments you need to so they look even.

3. Working left to right, attach your first button with a generous dab of fabric glue. Keep gluing buttons down, one at a time, following the pattern.

4. Repeat steps 1 through 3 to make your second curtain. Let them dry completely.

5. Clip on curtain rings to the top edge, spacing them about 4 inches apart, to hang your curtains.

button
KITCHEN SET

Techniques

HAND-SEWING,
MACHINE SEWING *(SEW CUTE APRON)*

The vintage-inspired pieces are perfect for cooking and crafting alike. Embellish a 1940s apron or a plain oven mitt with buttons for a quick pick-me-up, and keep a little wool felt pincushion and scissors close at hand for sewing up a storm in style.

You'll Need

Needle and thread

Scissors

Fabric marking pen

Plain oven mitt

One large button

Ten smaller buttons

ZIGZAG OVEN MITT

1. Hand-sew your large button in the middle of your oven mitt, about an inch below the wrist opening. Be sure to sew your buttons on well above the hand area, where you'll be touching hot pans, so as not to damage them.

2. Use your fabric pen to mark a zigzag pattern on each side of the large button. Arrange your small buttons, five on each side, slightly spaced so that you like the look of the design. Hand-sew each one on.

You'll Need

Your favorite small scissors

Sewing machine (optional)

Needle and thread

Pinking shears

One new or vintage apron

Three buttons of any style

Felt for pincushion: two 4-inch by 4-inch pieces

Polyfill stuffing for the pincushion

2½ yards narrow ⅛-inch ribbon

SEW CUTE APRON

1. Spread out your apron and mark placement for two buttons centered where your hipbones would sit, or where it seems comfortable for your sewing accessories to hang.

2. Hand-stitch both buttons through all layers.

3. Cut ribbon about 20 inches long. Tie knot and thread though the handle of your favorite small sewing scissors. Hang tied end from one button sewed to waistband. The ribbons in the photograph are shown shortened.

4. Cut second length of ribbon, also about 20 inches long, and fold in half. To begin creating your pincushion, sandwich the ribbon ends between the two layers of felt.

5. Sew squares together with a ¼-inch to ½-inch seam allowance, stitching over the ribbon ends and enclosing them inside. Leave a small opening and stuff. Sew closed. Use pinking shears to trim the decorative edge on all sides.

6. Sew a button in the center of the pincushion through all layers, pulling the thread tight. Knot and bury ends, making the pincushion tufted. Hang the finished pincushion on the other button on the waistband.

· By Amy Karol ·

flowered
TABLE SET

Dress up your table with embellished placemats and seasonal napkin rings in a color palette that you especially like.

Techniques

GLUING,
WIREWORK *(FOUR SEASONS NAPKIN RINGS)*

Tips

For the napkin rings, wrapped floral wire is the key to making them both sturdy and adjustable. You could also try stringing the buttons on elastic thread, or attaching the button vignettes to your own napkin rings using glue or floral tape.

You'll Need
(for one placemat)

Hot glue gun

One woven or fabric placemat

Two large wooden shank buttons

14 smaller plastic or wooden sew-through buttons

BLOSSOM PLACEMAT

1. Plug in your hot glue gun so it's ready to use. Set your placemat down and arrange your buttons in flower formation, with seven small buttons around one larger one. (I placed mine in the lower left corner.)

2. When you like the placement, lift the large center button up and attach it with a generous dab of hot glue. Now attach the smaller petal buttons, one at a time, around it.

3. Repeat to glue down your second blossom.

You'll Need

Craft glue

Felt or fabric scraps

An assortment of wrapped floral wire (I used a spool of 32 gauge and a package of 20 gauge)

Floral tape (optional)

An assortment of buttons in seasonal colors

Pencil

FOUR SEASONS NAPKIN RINGS

SPRING BLOOM:

1. Cut several leaves out of wool felt/fabric and poke a small hole at the base, then string your leaves and a large shank button onto an 8-inch piece of floral wire that has been curved into a circle (you can shape it with your fingers or around a small drinking glass).

2. Using your 32-gauge wire, twist little springy shoots around a pencil to come out from under the bloom. Glue down any wiggly spots.

SUMMER PENNY CANDY:

1. Using a 12-inch piece of 32-gauge wire or elastic thread, string buttons, tying them as you go.

2. Wind the wire ends together or tie off the elastic at the desired ring size, and trim the excess. Sew-through buttons also work well with this project.

AUTUMN BERRY:

1. Cut flower shapes out of wool felt/fabric and make small holes in the center to fit around the shank of your button.

2. Pull 3-inch pieces of 32-gauge wire through the shank of the individual buttons, bending the length in two and twisting together. Twist them all together to make a small corsage.

3. Glue or twist the entire arrangement onto a 6-inch piece of heavier wire that has been bent into a circle. You could also use floral tape to attach.

WINTER WHITES:

1. Cut an 8-inch piece of 20-gauge wire and bend it into an open circle. Thread white shank buttons on until nearly full and twist together the ends. Flip the wreath and glue at each shank.

2. Cut a 4-inch piece of 20- or 32-gauge wire and bend into a U-shape. Bend small hooks into each end. Attach the loops to the back side of the wreath to make the ring.

· By Melissa Frantz ·

dinner
PARTY SET

This coordinating set of wineglass charms and embellished cloth napkins makes it easy to keep track of which glass and which spot at the table belongs to each guest. It's a nice gift idea, too— just choose colors or styles that your host or hostess especially likes. You'll just need four sets of two matching or similar buttons to make both projects.

Techniques

HAND-SEWING *(BUTTONED NAPKINS)*,
BUTTON DANGLES *(WINEGLASS CHARMS)*

Tips

If you don't have two identical buttons to use for a set, just use two that are the same color so they're still easy to spot. It's also best to use machine-washable buttons for this project, like plastic instead of wood or painted glass.

You'll Need

Needle and thread

Four assorted vintage buttons

Four cloth napkins

1. Choose a spot on the lower left corner of your first napkin, about an inch from the side and bottom edges, and stitch your first button securely there. Knot the back.

2. Repeat with your next three napkins and buttons to complete the set.

WINEGLASS CHARMS

You'll Need

Pliers
....
Four assorted vintage buttons
....
24-gauge gold wire
....
Four gold eyepins, 2 inches to 3 inches long
....
Marker or pen

1. Create a button dangle with each button, closing the outer loop.

2. Curve your first eyepin around the pen or marker to form a circle. Clip the wire about ⅛ inch past the eyepin loop and create a 90° bend. (This will click into the loop to secure the circle around your wineglass.) Slip your first button onto the circle you just created.

3. Repeat step 2 to make the other three wineglass charms.

button
BATH SET

If you have houseguests coming to stay, why not personalize their set of washcloths and towels with a bright-colored button and ribbon design, so that each person has an instantly recognizable motif, like the Dinner Party Set? (See page 122.) You can also decorate a bath towel, pillowcase, or any other household necessities to match if you like.

(See page 122.)

Techniques

HAND-SEWING,
GLUING *(FLOWER GARDEN HAND TOWEL)*

Tips

Be sure to choose machine-washable buttons and ribbons for this project.

You'll Need

Scissors

Fray Check

Machine-washable fabric glue

Needle and thread

Plain hand towel

12 inches of ⅛-inch ribbon

Three buttons

FLOWER GARDEN HAND TOWEL

1. Cut your ribbon into these lengths: one 3 inches, two 2 inches, and eight about ¼ inch (I randomized my short pieces a bit.) Apply Fray Check to the raw ends of the ribbon pieces.

2. Arrange your ribbon pieces on the front of the towel to suggest a flower garden—I placed mine about ½ inch apart, with the tallest stem in the middle and a symmetrical grouping of the shorter stems around it. Add your buttons to the top of the three tallest ribbons to see how they will look.

3. When you are pleased with the arrangement, glue the ribbons down with fabric glue and let them dry. When they are set, hand-stitch your buttons over the tops of the tall stems.

You'll Need

Scissors

Needle and thread

Fray Check

Straight pins

Plain washcloth

3 inches of ⅛-inch ribbon

One button

FLOWER LOOP WASHCLOTH

1. Choose a corner of your washcloth and mark a spot ½ inch in from the edge. Put a drop of Fray Check on the ends of the ribbon. Double it into a loop for hanging your washcloth, and pin it in place there.

2. Stitch it down to secure it and then place your button over the raw edges. Hand-sew the button down, covering the ribbon.

embellished button
P I L L O W S

Monogram a plain pillow, or accentuate a polka-dot patterned one with a big covered button to make a tuft shape—you can start from scratch or work with one you already have. If you'd like to sew a pillow cover yourself, just add 1 inch to the measurement of your pillow form and cut your fabric into squares that size.

Techniques

HAND-SEWING, MACHINE SEWING, COVERED BUTTONS *(POLKA DOTS GALORE)*

You'll Need

Paper and pencil

Scissors

Needle and thread

Fabric marking pen

Embroidery hoop

Sewing machine (recommended)

Iron

Two 13½-inch-square pieces of fabric or premade pillow cover

12-inch-square pillow form

Assorted or identical buttons (I used 40 small shell buttons to make my S)

I N I T I A L E D   P I L L O W

1. Choose a font that you like, or hand-draw your initial on paper. When you like the look of it, use your marking pen to draw it in the center of one piece of fabric or on the front of your pillow cover. Change it for size or style once it's on the fabric—a few drops of water take the marks right off. Use an embroidery hoop to keep the fabric taut and easy to work with.

2. Arrange your buttons all along the letter's perimeter. When you like the spacing, start hand-sewing each button down, working from one side to the other, until you have sewn them all on. Knot securely at the end of the thread.

3. Press the fabric and pin the two pieces together, right sides facing, around three sides, leaving the bottom edge open. Machine or hand-sew the three sides using a ½-inch seam allowance. Clip the corners and turn the pillow sleeve right side out.

4. Press the raw edges down ½ inch toward the wrong side of the fabric. Slip the pillow inside the sleeve and pin the folded edge together.

5. Machine or hand-sew the last seam to finish the pillow cover.

You'll Need

Scissors

Straight pins

Sewing machine (recommended)

Needle and thread

Iron

Fabric marking pen

Two 15½-inch-square pieces of polka-dot fabric

14-inch-square pillow

One 1½-inch covered button in a coordinating color

One sew-through button in a coordinating color

POLKA DOTS GALORE

1. Construct your pillow cover the same way as the Initialed Pillow in steps 3 through 5 (see page 126).

2. Mark the center of your pillow front. Bring your needle and thread all the way through your pillow there, from front to back, and then stitch back through again. Repeat this twice more to form a tuft. On your last loop through, stitch on your sew-through button on the back.

3. Sew your large covered button in the center of the tuft on the front. Knot your thread securely in the back.

button
DECOR

Decorate your house with simple, pretty button arrangements
—these projects are a fun way to use a handful of favorites
and make yourself something that's not so much functional
as fun.

Techniques

GLUING *(COLOR WHEEL MIRROR)*,
WIREWORK *(BUTTON COLLAGE)*

You'll Need

Cement glue

Wire cutters (if you are using any
buttons with shanks)

Plain 5-inch round mirror

Assorted buttons in an array of
colors (I used 16 buttons, each
about the size of a quarter)

COLOR WHEEL MIRROR

1. Go through your buttons and arrange them around the edge of your mirror
   in a color wheel formation, rearranging them to flow nicely from one hue to
   the next.

2. If you are using any buttons with shanks, remove them so that they lie flat.

3. Starting with any one button, lift it off the mirror and apply a generous dab of
   glue there. Press it back down to set.

4. Repeat all the way around the mirror and let the glue dry completely.

You'll Need

1-inch foam brush

Awl

Acid-free glue stick

Wire cutters

One 10-inch by 10-inch canvas

Acrylic paint

16 2-inch by 2-inch scraps of fabric, cut, ripped, or trimmed with pinking shears

14 vintage buttons

24- or 26-gauge wire

BUTTON COLLAGE

1. Paint canvas with two coats of acrylic paint and let dry.

2. Arrange fabrics in a grid in a pleasing way, keeping prints and colors well balanced. Pick buttons to go with individual scraps and lay in place, leaving a couple of fabric scraps button-less.

3. With wire cutters, cut fourteen 4-inch lengths of wire and set aside.

4. Starting in upper left corner, pick up button and fabric piece and apply glue evenly around edges on back of fabric piece. Press smoothly to canvas.

5. Replace button on fabric piece in original position. Pierce fabric and canvas with the awl through each hole in button. Pick up button and thread wire through holes so that the ends of wire come out of back of button. Insert ends of wire through holes in fabric canvas gently, without disturbing other unsecured buttons on canvas. Push button onto canvas, bending wires beneath. (You will twist the ends of these wires together securely once you've wired on all the buttons.)

6. Repeat steps 4 and 5 for each scrap of fabric/button combination. When all buttons have been wired to canvas, turn canvas over and twist wires on back to secure. Trim wires so that canvas lies flat.

· By Alicia Paulson ·

· chapter ·

6

ACCESSORIES, EMBELLISHMENTS & GIFTS

button **HAIR CLIPS**
button **HAIRCOMB**
button embellished **TOP**
button embellished **SKIRT**
button embellished **HANDBAG**
button embellished **MARKET BAG**
button **STATIONERY SET**
button **JARS**
button **HOLIDAY DECORATIONS**
button **TOYS**

button
HAIR CLIPS

Add colorful buttons to plain hairpins or clips for a quick dose of style. These make a pretty gift, too!

Technique
GLUING *(SHINY SET)*

Tips
Make sure that the buttons you choose aren't too heavy for the clip or bobby pin you're embellishing, or your new hair accessory may slide right out of your hair.

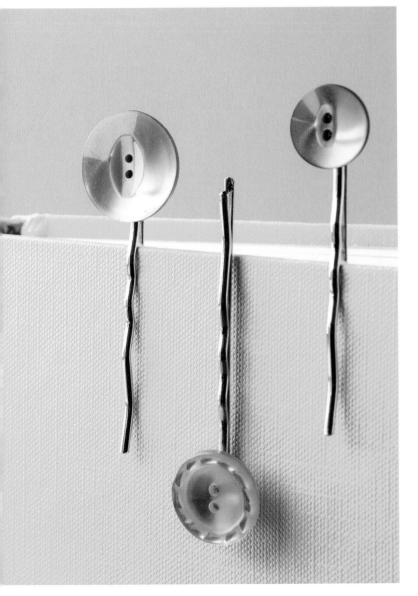

SHINY SET

You'll Need

Cement glue

Sew-through buttons

Bobby pin blanks

Apply a dab of glue to a bobby pin blank and press the button onto it, face up. Let dry completely. Repeat to make as many hairpins as you'd like.

E ⏱

FLOWER CLIPS

You'll Need

Industrial-strength glue

Button of your choice

Metal flower charm

Blank hairclip

1. Layer the button and flower so you like the pairing and glue them securely together. Let them dry completely.

2. Glue the button flower to the flat space at the end of the hair clip and let that dry completely, too.

button
HAIRCOMB

These embellished combs are perfect for showing off a row of your favorite buttons. Whether you make one large one to anchor an updo or a pair of smaller side combs, they're a lovely accessory to wear out and about.

Techniques

SEWING *(BAKELITE)*,
GLUING *(ROW OF SPARKLES)*

You'll Need

One card of silk beading cord (pre-threaded with a twisted wire needle)

Scissors

Cement glue

Three large buttons

Four smaller buttons in a coordinating color

Blank haircomb

BAKELITE

1. Working from left to right, arrange your buttons in an order you like. (I alternated small and large ones.)

2. Choose your first button for the left side of your comb. Bring your beading cord from back to front between the first two teeth of the comb, leaving a tail. Then loop it over the top of the comb to meet the other end, and knot them tightly together at the back. Slip the first button onto the cord and stitch it down securely so it stays in place on the far left of the comb, wrapping the cord again behind it.

3. Wrap the cord between the teeth once or twice working from left to right. Now stitch on your first large button, stitching through it twice to hold it securely. Continue wrapping the cord between each tooth of the comb behind the button.

4. Repeat steps 2 and 3 to add the next five buttons.

5. When you have reached the right side of the comb, tie another knot.

6. Add a drop of glue to each knot to secure them, and clip the excess cord away.

You'll Need

Hot glue gun

Eight larger rhinestone buttons

Six smaller rhinestone buttons

Two plain hair combs

ROW OF SPARKLES

1. Arrange your buttons in a pattern that you like. (I alternated between large and small.)

2. Apply a generous dab of hot glue to the far left of your first comb. Push the first button into it so that the glue surrounds the shank before it cools.

3. Repeat step 2 to add your next six buttons, and then make your second comb the same way.

button
embellished
T O P

Add a flurry of buttons to a plain shirt to create a brooch-like effect. Have fun playing with the combination of colors, textures, and sizes of buttons. You can try out different themes, like bright colors, contrast colors, earthy, pastel, same color but different size buttons . . . the sky is the limit. And any shirt can work.

Technique
HAND-SEWING

You'll Need

Sewing needle and thread

Scissors

One large center button

Seven smaller buttons to arrange around it

Smaller buttons for cuffs (if desired)

1. Place your shirt on a flat surface and arrange your buttons as you like. (I put my biggest central button on the upper right side of my shirt, and added seven smaller ones around it like the petals of a flower.)

2. Hand-stitch the buttons on, one at a time.

3. Replace the plain buttons on each cuff with fancier ones (if you like).

BUTTON CORSAGE

You'll Need

Sewing needle

Thread

Scissors

Assorted buttons

Shirt (scoop neck or V-neck works nicely, or sew the corsage on the collar of a button-down shirt)

1. Lay out your shirt on a flat surface. Choose a few buttons from your stash and place them on your shirt in the layout you prefer. Play with the number, size, color, and layout of the buttons until you like the combination. (If you need help remembering the layout, place the buttons on a piece of paper in the order that you will sew them on the shirt, or snap a quick photo.)

2. Choose your starting point and sew the buttons on the shirt in a sequential order. As you are traveling between buttons, use a tiny stitch here and there so that you don't have big stitches on the back of the shirt. Also, be careful not to pull your thread too tight to avoid puckering the fabric.

3. When you have reached the last button, make a knot and cut your thread.

· By Rebecca Pearcy ·

button
embellished
S K I R T

Do you have a few tired or plain skirts hanging in the back of your closet that you never wear? Some easy embellishments will spice them up and move them into heavy rotation.

Techniques

**HAND-SEWING,
MACHINE-SEWING** *(OPTIONAL)*

Tips

Meredith MacDonald says, "Another variation is to sew the buttons onto a grosgrain ribbon, and then sew the ribbon directly to the skirt. And be sure to choose a skirt that is sturdy enough to withstand the extra weight of the buttons without affecting its fit or drape."

You'll Need

Sewing machine (if you want to use one for stitching on the trims)

Needle and thread to attach the buttons

Iron

Straight pins

Plain skirt

Trim, such as ribbon or rick-rack (enough to go all the way around the bottom of the skirt)

Assorted or matching vintage buttons (I used 12 pink buttons)

F L I R T Y   S K I R T

1. Press the skirt and the trim with a hot iron.

2. Figure out how you want to arrange your buttons and trim on your skirt.

3. Once you have determined your configuration, pin the trim to the skirt.

4. Sew the trim to the skirt using a sewing machine or needle and thread.

5. Sew the buttons on.

· *By Mariko Fujinaka* ·

You'll Need

Needle and thread

Plain skirt

Assortment of buttons (for my skirt, I used 26)

Ruler or measuring tape

Scissors

MOLLY'S BUTTON SKIRT

1. Measure your skirt. Determine how many buttons you want to use and how far apart you'd like them placed. For my 18-inch skirt, I measured approximately 1½ inches from each button center to accommodate different-size buttons.

2. Arrange the buttons on a table first to make sure you like the arrangement.

3. Starting from either the hem or the waist, sew the buttons on. For additional security, knot the thread and cut it off, starting with a new thread every few buttons. If you choose not to do this step, be extra careful when washing the skirt, and consider putting it in a mesh laundry bag in the washing machine.

4. Measure from the center of the button to the next button center and continue sewing.

5. Repeat on the other side.

· By Meredith MacDonald ·

button embellished
HANDBAG

Embellish a simple handbag with buttons and your favorite fabrics or ribbons to create your own gorgeous take on color and style. Whether you sew your own purse from scratch or add pretty touches to a premade bag, you'll never see another one quite like it.

Techniques

**HAND-SEWING,
MACHINE SEWING** *(OPTIONAL)*

You'll Need

Iron

Circle templates (bowls and cups work well)

Fabric marking pen

Seam ripper

Needle and thread

Sewing machine (optional—may be necessary if bag is lined)

Plain cotton purse

Prewashed fabric remnants

Iron-on adhesive (I used Heat'n Bond Lite)

Approximately 80–100 assorted small buttons

BIRDS AND BUTTONS BAG

1. Using templates, trace circle shapes of varying sizes onto the backside of your fabric remnants. If you are framing an image printed on your fabric, remember to leave an extra ½ inch all around so that the buttons don't cover the part of the fabric you want to see.

2. Cut out fabric circles. Cut a second circle from the iron-on adhesive for each one. Following package instructions, iron adhesive to fabric. Place fabric circles onto purse and arrange them as desired. Use the circle templates and marking pen to trace circles onto the bag. Once you've found a design you like, peel paper backing from fabric circles and iron them to the purse.

3. If your bag has a lining, you'll want to seam-rip the top stitches of the lining to release it. This way you won't have to sew through two layers of fabric to attach the buttons, and when you re-stitch the lining in place, none of the messy threads will show inside the bag (or risk getting caught on your purse contents and coming loose). Pin the lining to the back of the purse so it won't get in your way.

4. Arrange your buttons on the purse first to get an idea of what you like. Next, sew on buttons all around the appliquéd fabric circles as desired, making sure to pull thread tight. To finish, re-stitch the lining in place.

· By Linda Permann ·

You'll Need

Sewing machine

Fabric scissors

Iron and ironing board

Sewing needle and thread

Chalk marker

Your favorite basic purse pattern

Fabric for the exterior and lining (refer to pattern)

Fusible interfacing like Decor-Bond (same amount as exterior fabric)

One set of magnetic snaps

Velvet ribbon (I used about 24 inches)

Satin ribbon (I used about 12 inches)

Matching thread

Eight 5/8-inch sew-through buttons

Two 1 1/8-inch shank buttons

Two 1 5/8-inch shank buttons

SHADES OF GRAY EVENING BAG

1. Cut out pattern pieces. Fuse the interfacing to the wrong side of the fabric you are using for the exterior of the bag.

2. Cut out exterior bag pieces and straps from the fused fabric and cut out your lining pieces.

3. Place the ribbons in a pleasing arrangement onto exterior bag pieces. (I did diagonal lines but you can really do anything.)

4. Using your chalk marker, mark the placement of the ribbons onto the fabric. Use your sewing machine to edge-stitch the ribbons in place.

5. Place the buttons on top of the ribbon and mark placement with the chalk marker. Hand-sew them into place.

6. Stitch straps, turn right side out and press. Stitch straps onto bag.

7. Stitch up bag and then lining, leaving a 4-inch opening on one side seam.

8. Iron a 3-inch-square scrap of fusible interfacing onto the wrong side of lining on each side where the magnetic snaps will go. This will prevent the snaps from tearing out.

9. Install magnetic snaps according to instructions. Make sure to place them at least 1¼ inches below top edge of lining.

10. Leaving the lining inside out and the bag right side out, insert bag into lining. Stitch all around the top edge of the bag.

11. Turn bag right side out through the opening you left in the lining. Tuck in raw edges and topstitch the opening shut.

12. Push the lining down into the bag and slide the bag onto the nose of the ironing board. Working your way around, press the top edge of the bag flat. Be careful not to press directly on top of the magnetic snaps or your bag will get a shine mark that will be impossible to remove.

· By Nicole Vasbinder ·

button embellished
MARKET BAG

You can use these ideas to embellish market bags that you already have, of course, but if you'd like to sew one of these totes from scratch, Diane and Kristin have patterns and full instructions on the buttonitupbook.com Web site for their Button Sampler and Spring Roll Delight bags. Why the unusual name for Kristin's bag? She says, "When it's rolled up, it reminds me so much of the spring rolls served at my favorite Thai restaurant."

Techniques

**HAND-SEWING,
MACHINE SEWING** *(OPTIONAL)*

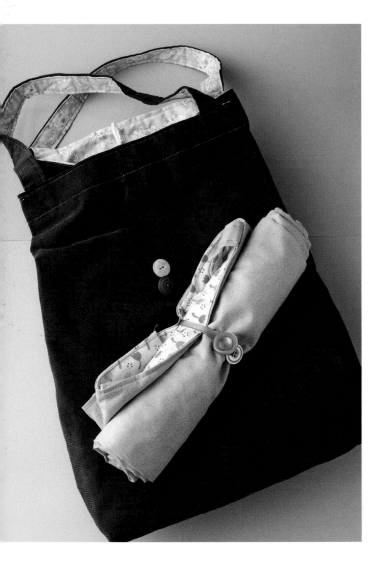

SPRING ROLL DELIGHT

You'll Need

Needle and thread

Scissors

Straight pins

Tote-style market bag

Two buttons, ⅝ inch or larger

7 inches of ¼-inch-wide ribbon or elastic

1. Following the instructions online, create your tote bag, or choose a bag you already have, and lay it out flat.

2. Fold the ribbon or elastic in half and create a loop with it, pinning it to the center top of the front side of the bag, between the straps. Hand-sew it in place.

3. Now roll your bag up from the bottom to the top. Mark where the loop extends to the other side of your bag.

4. Sew your closure button at your marked spot and add another button directly above it.

5. Roll your bag up, folding the straps inside, and fasten it with the loop!

· *By Kristin Roach* ·

BUTTON SAMPLER TOTE

You'll Need

Needle and thread

Scissors

Fabric glue

Tote-style market bag

21 buttons in assorted sizes (for this design, you'll need seven groups of three buttons, in graduated sizes)

1. Following the instructions posted on buttonitupbook.com, create your tote bag, or choose a bag you already have and lay it out flat. Place your buttons on the front, and move them around until you have a configuration you like.

2. The key to this design is in how precisely you can place your buttons. You want them to line up straight, with all the holes facing the same way. Tack the buttons in place before sewing by putting a small amount of fabric glue on the back of each one. Be sure not to get any glue behind the holes in the buttons, and don't let any ooze out from the edges of the buttons. A tiny drop will be enough. Allow glue to dry, preferably overnight.

3. Using a hand-sewing needle and contrasting thread, sew all the buttons to the bag.

· *By Diane Gilleland* ·

button
STATIONERY SET

Make up a pretty set of personalized embroidered cards to send out, and embellish a plain pencil cup with rows of buttons and a favorite patterned paper. This set would be a lovely gift, or fun for you to keep.

Techniques

BACKSTITCHING *(BUTTON BOUQUET CARDS),*
WIRE LOOPING *(PRETTY PENCIL CUP)*

Tips

Kayte says, "When embroidering on paper, always make holes for the embroidery pattern before you stitch through the paper. Make sure to use a very sharp embroidery needle to make the holes. It's easy to make multiples of these cards: I like to gather and prep all my materials first and then assemble all the cards at once."

You'll Need

Spray adhesive

X-acto® knife

Ruler and cutting mat

Paper scissors

Decorative scissors with scalloped edge

One sheet 8½-inch by 11-inch cardstock (A)

One sheet 8½-inch by 11-inch cardstock in contrasting color (B)

Small scrap of wallpaper or patterned paper

Three or four buttons in assorted shapes and colors

Pencil

Embroidery floss in desired colors

Embroidery needle

One A2 envelope

BUTTON BOUQUET CARDS

1. Fold cardstock A in half lengthwise. Cut in half with an X-acto knife, ruler, and cutting mat (so you have two pieces of cardstock that are each 4¼ inches by 5½ inches) and set card aside.

2. Measure and cut out a 4-inch by 5¼-inch piece of contrast-color cardstock B with your X-acto knife. Set aside the other halves of your cardstock for a future card project.

3. Decide where you want to place your wallpaper scrap on cardstock B. Cut a small rectangle with the scallop-edged scissors. Affix to cardstock B with spray adhesive.

4. Lightly draw stems, leaves, and flower petals freehand on cardstock B with a pencil.

5. With embroidery needle, poke holes along the pencil lines as a guide for embroidery. Erase pencil lines.

6. Sew buttons to the cardstock for the centers of the flowers and knot on back.

7. Backstitch through the premade holes with three strands of embroidery floss in desired colors and knot on back.

8. When embroidery is complete, affix your button flower card piece to cardstock A, with spray adhesive and allow to dry. Use your A2 envelope with your card.

· By Kayte Terry ·

You'll Need

Pliers

Scissors or paper cutter

Double-stick tape

Mesh pencil cup

24-gauge craft wire

Assorted buttons in the same color family

Decorative paper

PRETTY PENCIL CUP

1. Cut a 2-foot piece of craft wire and form a wrapped loop at one end. Choose a spot ½ inch down from the top of the pencil cup and thread the wire through, from the inside to the outside, and slip the wire tail through your first button. Bring it back down through the opposite buttonhole and thread it back into the cup, slipping it through the wire loop to secure it.

2. Add the second button next to it, weaving the wire through the same way and pulling it taut as you go. I alternated larger and smaller buttons all the way around the top of the cup.

3. When you add your last button, wind the wire through the mesh a few times to secure it and clip the end.

4. Now measure from just below the center of the buttons to the same distance at the bottom of the cup—mine measured 3½ inches. This interval will be where you put your decorative paper. Now measure the circumference of the cup (mine measured 12 inches) and cut a piece of paper to fit, with an overlap of ½ inch. My paper was 3½ inches tall and 12½ inches long.

5. Put a piece of double-stick tape on one short end of the paper and carefully place the paper around the cup, slipping it under the button row at the top. Press the other end of the paper over the tape to join them.

6. Add another row of buttons at the bottom as you did in steps 1 through 3.

button JARS

Sure, jars and canisters are perfect for storing buttons, but why not decorate them with buttons on the outside as well? Glue an assortment of buttons onto glass jars, or use magnets to hold your crafty to-dos and reminders on a neatly repurposed paint can.

Technique

GLUING

Tips

Instead of using paper to cover the canister, you can paint it using semi-gloss latex paint.

ARRAY OF BUTTONS

You'll Need

Hot glue gun

Empty jar with lid

One large button

Assorted smaller buttons in the same color family (I used 52 red buttons for my large jar, and nine medium lavender buttons and 22 small shell buttons for my small one)

Pliers

24-gauge wire

1. Place your large button in the center of the jar lid and glue it down securely. For my smaller jar, I also surrounded the large button with 10 small shell buttons.

2. Begin gluing smaller buttons on the sides of the jar. For my larger jar, I randomized the button placement, and for my smaller one, I added two lavender buttons to each side in a diagonal, and three shell buttons in an opposite-facing diagonal.

3. Let cool completely.

4. Create a button dangle with one last button and embellish the opener with it.

PENCIL CANISTER WITH BUTTON MAGNETS

You'll Need

Scissors

Double-stick tape or adhesive

Silicone glue

Decorative paper

Empty paint can or other metal canister

Vintage buttons

Magnets

1. Measure the length and circumference of your canister. Add ½ inch to the length and cut paper.

2. Apply double-stick tape or adhesive along the top and bottom of the paper.

3. Put paper on canister, making sure the paper is adhered to canister.

4. Glue one magnet onto the back of each vintage button. Let dry for several hours.

5. Your pencil cup with button magnets is ready for use!

· By Sally J. Shim ·

button
HOLIDAY
DECORATIONS

Vintage buttons certainly make pretty embellishments any time of year, but there is something especially nice about decorating with them for holidays. Wire buttons onto a plain wreath in your favorite colors, or create a glistening button tree for your table.

Techniques

WIRE LOOPING, GLUING *(RED AND GOLD WREATH)*

Tips

Sarah says, "To embellish the tree, if you use shank buttons, you will have to use tweezers to bend the silk pins to hold the buttons to the Styrofoam cone. The addition of rhinestones, pearls, earrings, etc., will change the look of your tree. Make your tree with only sew-through buttons for a very different look."

You'll Need

Pliers

Hot glue gun

Scissors

Plain wreath

Assortment of buttons in your choice of colors (I used three large red ones, four medium red ones, and eight medium gold ones in two patterns)

24-gauge floral wire (to match the color of the wreath)

18 inches of 1½-inch-wide ribbon

RED AND GOLD WREATH

1. Arrange your buttons around the wreath in the order you like. I chose to place large buttons in roughly the 12, 3, and 9 o'clock positions around the circle, and filled in between them with a symmetrical pattern of the smaller buttons, alternating red and gold. I left a large space at the bottom center for my ribbon.

2. When you like the design, cut a 2-foot piece of floral wire and make a wrapped loop at one end. Loop it around the wreath near the first button (I started at the 7 o'clock position and worked left to right) and then thread it through that first button, catching it securely. Wrap it again to the side of the button.

3. Add the second button the same way, and continue around the wreath, looping once between each button.

4. When you reach your last button, wrap the wire tail around the wreath several times, tucking the end to the back of the wreath.

5. Tie a bow with your ribbon, angling edges if you like, and hot-glue it in place at the bottom of the wreath.

(M)

You'll Need

Tweezers

Double-stick tape

Craft glue (optional)

Styrofoam cone, 9 inches tall

Corsage pins (fancy pearl-headed pins), at least 200

Silk pins (tiny silver pins with flat heads), at least 500

Approximately 600 buttons, which is roughly a pound (I used vintage buttons, which are readily available at flea markets)

Other assorted baubles like rhinestones, vintage earrings, etc.

Glass beads of all shapes and sizes, including seed beads (you need as many glass beads as buttons)

Pearls

One piece of fabric to cover the cone (I used pink)

One piece of wool felt, 7 inches by 7 inches

BUTTON TREE

1. Wrap the cone in fabric. Using the silk pins, pin the excess fabric on the top and bottom down. Pin along the side seam of the fabric also.

2. Start sticking on buttons with the silk pins. In order to keep most of the buttons on the pin you will need to put first a bead, or several beads, on the pin, and then the button. You could skip the beads if your buttons have holes small enough to hold on tight by the pin alone. I did the first layer of buttons in all white buttons, trying to keep larger ones near the bottom and smaller ones near the top. You can glue each button on in addition to using the pins, but you may have to work faster as the layers of dried glue could make it difficult to insert pins later on.

3. Start adding on the second layer of buttons, this time using all your special buttons, earrings, and other bits and bobs. Use the corsage pins and/or the silk pins with prettier beads, because you will be able to see the pins from this layer. Try to put the second layer of buttons in between the places from the first layer, where the fabric is still showing.

4. When the tree starts to look full, I suggest adding at least 20 more buttons. It looks better when it is as full as you can get it.

5. Fill in the still empty-looking spaces with pearls, rhinestones, and beads, no buttons this time. Stack them on pins, and start filling in the spaces where buttons wouldn't fit in step 4.

6. Choose something for a tree topper. I used a vintage clip-on earring, which I attached with a pearl-headed pin. Pin the topper to the top.

7. Cut out a scalloped skirt for the bottom, and attach it to the bottom of the cone with permanent double-stick tape.

· By Sarah Johner ·

button
TOYS

Make a fun little toy with buttons—they lend themselves to become eyes and features, or neatly wired arms and legs, so easily! Find a pattern for the owl toy on buttonitupbook.com.

Techniques

COVERED BUTTONS *(BIG-EYED OWL),*
HAND-SEWING, WIREWORK *(WOODLAND FAIRY)*

Tips

*Remember, if you are making your toy for a small child, be sure to sew or wire your buttons on **very** securely so they can't be pulled off or swallowed.*

You'll Need

Scissors

Straight pins

Needle and thread

Sewing machine (recommended)

Two 8½-inch by 11-inch pieces of wool felt

Remnant of contrast fabric for eyes

Two 1½-inch buttons to cover

Six small triangle-shaped buttons

Fiberfill stuffing

BIG-EYED OWL

1. Cut out two identical owl shapes and pin them together, leaving an opening at the bottom.

2. Machine or hand-sew close to the edge all around the perimeter, backstitching before and after the opening.

3. Stuff the owl with fiberfill and then pin the opening closed and machine or hand sew it.

4. Make your covered buttons and stitch them onto the face for eyes.

5. Hand-sew the triangular buttons in groups of three for claws.

You'll Need

Acrylic paint and small brush, or permanent markers for drawing the fairy's face

All-purpose glue (I used Aleene's Tacky Glue)

Long sewing needle

30 sew-through shirt buttons in assorted colors

30 white sew-through shirt buttons

Two small shank buttons for fairy hands

One small glittery button for top of fairy hat

Two small yarn pompoms for fairy body

Six strands of yarn for braids

One 20 mm wooden bead for fairy head

18-inch 28-gauge wire

Artificial flower with multiple petals and green plastic base (that you can take apart for hat and skirt)

WOODLAND FAIRY

1. Paint or draw a face on the wooden bead and allow to dry.

2. Hold yarn pieces in a hank and knot together in the center. Braid together on either side of the center knot and secure each braid at the end.

3. Once the head is dry, glue the braids to it, with the center knot near the center hole of the bead head (it is okay if it covers the hole on top of the bead a bit, but don't block the hole completely with glue).

4. Take apart the artificial flower so you have several colored petals and a green leaf.

5. Thread the wire through your needle and then thread 15 multicolored buttons onto the wire, leaving a 3-inch tail. Run the needle back through the holes opposite the ones you came out in the buttons and wrap the tail around the top so the buttons make a secure column: your first multicolored fairy stocking.

6. Run the needle and wire through the center of one pompom, then through the center hole of a colored flower petal. Run the needle through the center of the second pompom, to secure the skirt between the two. Once through the second pompom, run the needle through the fairy head and braid, then the center of a green flower petal to make the hat. To secure, run the needle through the center of the small hat button, back down through another hole in the button, and follow the needle's path back down until it comes out the bottom pompom near to your first fairy leg.

7. Thread 15 more multicolored buttons on the wire to make your fairy's second striped stocking. Run the wire back up through the buttons and pull the wire nice and tight so the leg buttons are flush with the bottom of the pompom body. Wrap the wire around the top of the leg a few times to secure.

8. Run the needle back up through the center of the body, bringing it out on the right side of the body just above the skirt. Run your needle through 15 white buttons and then run it through the shank of one of the small buttons you've chosen for the fairy hands. Come out the other side of the shank and run the needle back through the second hole in the white buttons. (If they have four holes, then come out diagonally from the one you came out). Pull tight so the hand shank pulls the arm taut and the arm pulls up flush with the body.

9. Push the needle through to the left side of the body and repeat step 7 to make the left arm and hand. Wrap the end of the wire around the join between the body and the arm to secure, and then cut the wire, burying any sharp ends deep in the pompom body.

10. Position your fairy's hat, head, and braids as you like them, and use small drops of glue to secure in place. Allow glue to dry, and then play!

· By Nancy Flynn ·

RESOURCES

Here are some of my favorite books on vintage buttons:

About Buttons: A Collector's Guide by Peggy Ann Osborne

The Button Lover's Book by Marilyn Green

Buttons by Diana Epstein and Millicent Safro

Buttons: The Collector's Guide to Selecting, Restoring, and Enjoying New and Vintage Buttons by Nancy Fink and Maryalice Ditzler

The Collector's Encyclopedia of Buttons by Sally C. Luscomb

And some recommended sources for buttons, jewelry findings, and craft supplies:

BERGER BEADS *(vintage and new jewelry materials)*
413 East 8th Street
Los Angeles, CA 90014
213-627-8783
www.bergerbeads.net

BRITEX FABRICS^{SM} *(buttons, fabric, and sewing supplies)*
146 Geary Street
San Francisco, CA 94108
415-392-2910
www.britexfabrics.com

THE BUTTON EMPORIUM
(new and vintage buttons and ribbons)
914 SW 11th Avenue
Portland, OR 97205
503-228-6372
www.buttonemporium.com

BUZZARD BRAND *(vintage and hand-cast buttons, craft and jewelry supplies)*
www.thebuzzardbrand.com

ELOXITE *(jewelry blanks, beads, and tools)*
307-322-3050
eloxite.com

EXCLUSIVE BUTTONS *(vintage buttons)*
10252 San Pablo Avenue
El Cerrito, CA 94530
510-524-5606

FIRE MOUNTAIN GEMS *(beads and jewelry supplies)*
800-355-2137
www.firemountaingems.com

GREAT BUTTONS *(new and vintage buttons)*
1030 Avenue of the Americas
New York, NY 10018
212-869-6811

M & J TRIMMING *(lace, ribbons, trims, and buttons)*
1008 Avenue of the Americas
New York, NY 10018
800-9-MJTRIM
www.mjtrim.com

METALLIFEROUS *(vintage and new beads, charms, and chains, plus tools and findings)*
34 West 46th Street
New York, NY 10036
888-944-0909
www.metalliferous.com

MICHAEL LEVINE INC. *(fabrics, buttons, and ribbons)*
920 South Maple Avenue
Los Angeles, CA 90015
213-622-6259
www.mlfabrics.net

RINGS AND THINGS *(metal and findings of all kinds)*
800-366-2156
www.rings-things.com

RIO GRANDE *(semiprecious, metal, and tools)*
800-545-6566
www.riogrande.com

TENDER BUTTONS *(vintage and antique buttons)*
143 East 62nd Street
New York, NY 10065
212-758-7004

TOHO SHOJI *(beads, chain, charms, and crystals)*
990 Avenue of the Americas, Suite 3
New York, NY 10018
212-868-7466
www.tohoshoji-ny.com

Don't forget to search Etsy (etsy.com) and eBay (ebay.com) for vintage buttons or any other specific things you're looking for, or browse a whole category. Estate sales, flea markets, antique fairs, and thrift stores are amazing resources for vintage pieces, too.

GUEST DESIGNERS

(p. 70)

CATHY CALLAHAN draws inspiration from crafts and design of the 1960s and '70s. She bases her projects on things she finds in her collection of vintage craft publications: cathyofcalifornia.com.

(p. 164)

NANCY FLYNN is the author of *Jeaneology: Crafty Ways to Reinvent Your Old Blues*, and co-editor of getcrafty.com. Find a chronicle of her crafty adventures at belleepoquewhimsy.com.

(p. 120)

MELISSA FRANTZ lives in Portland, Oregon, where she drinks too much coffee and sews as much as her two kids will allow. She blogs at allbuttonedup.typepad.com.

(p. 143)

MARIKO FUJINAKA lives in Portland, Oregon, with her understanding husband and demanding dog. She blogs about crafting, baking, and other exploits at supereggplant.com.

(p. 151)

DIANE GILLELAND, aka Sister Diane, produces CraftyPod (craftypod.com), a blog and bi-weekly podcast about Making Stuff. She also runs DIY Alert (diyalert.com), a Web site about all things crafty in Portland, Oregon.

(p. 160)

Both a crafter and a junker, **SARAH JOHNER** enjoys everything from sewing and button crafts to collecting vintage pottery. Find her blog, Making Projiks, The Misadventures of Mama & Jack, at mamanjackjack.blogspot.com.

(p. 116)

AMY KAROL lives in Portland, Oregon, with her three beautiful girls and husband and has always wanted a pet koala bear. She wrote *Bend-the-Rules Sewing: The Essential Guide to a Whole New Way to Sew*, and you can find her up to no good on her blog, angrychicken.typepad.com. For a slightly more organized view of her world, visit amykarol.com.

(p. 56)

LEAH KRAMER is the founder of craftster.org, an online community for fans of hip, modern craft projects. She's also the author of *The Craftster Guide to Nifty, Thrifty, and Kitschy Crafts*.

(p. 103)

CHRISTINA LOFF is a crafter and writer living in San Francisco. You can read about her adventures and creations at borrowedboughtstolen.blogspot.com.

(p. 144)

MEREDITH MACDONALD crafts and lives on the East Coast with her husband. Find her sewing, knitting, cooking, and Blythe doll adventures at paperdollygirl.com.

(p. 76)

TORIE NGUYEN makes and sells jewelry under the name Totinette (totinette.com), is a member of PDX Super Crafty (pdxsupercrafty.com), and co-organizes the Crafty Wonderland sale. When not crafting, she's a Realtor who runs a blog called I Love Portland Homes.

(p. 132)

ALICIA PAULSON dreams in calico and crochet hooks, and spends her days designing crafts in her home studio in Portland, Oregon. She is the author of *Stitched in Time: Memory-Keeping Projects to Sew and Share from the Creator of Posie Gets Cozy*.

(p. 141)

REBECCA PEARCY is the founder and designer of Queen Bee Creations. Find her products at boutiques throughout the U.S. and online at queenbee-creations.com.

(p. 74)

JENNIFER PERKINS is the author of *Naughty Secretary Club: Jewelry for the Working Girl*, Web mistress of jewelry Web site naughtysecretaryclub.com, and a member of the Austin Craft Mafia.

(p. 146)

LINDA PERMANN is a freelance writer and craft designer. She loves to sew, crochet, knit, and bake, and is always on the lookout for cookie tins full of old buttons. Read all about it at lindamade.wordpress.com.

(p. 64)

CHRISTY PETTERSON is a writer, crafter, PR specialist, avid coffee drinker, native Atlantan, roadie for her drummer of a husband, and all-around nice person. She is co-organizer of the Indie Craft Experience, a bi-annual craft market in Atlanta (ice-atlanta.com), co-editor of Get Crafty (getcrafty.com), and creator of the a bardis accessory line (abardis.com).

(p. 150)

KRISTIN ROACH enjoys the process of finding meaning and purpose in forgotten materials and experiences. Her work ranges from painting to pattern writing, but she always connects to material identity and process: kristinroach.wordpress.com.

(p. 157)

SALLY J. SHIM is the designer behind Shim + Sons, a home accessories and stationery design studio based in Portland, Oregon: shimandsons.com.

(p. 15)

LAURA STOKES produces her Buzzard Brand line of resin trinkets and jewelry in her Southern California studio. Her array of handmade and vintage findings are available at www.the buzzardbrand.com.

(p. 95)

AMANDA BLAKE SOULE is the author of *The Creative Family: How to Encourage Imagination and Nurture Family Connections*. She blogs at soulemama.com, where she writes about and photographs her days crafting, thrifting, and parenting three little ones on the coast of Maine.

(p. 152)

KAYTE TERRY is a crafter, stylist, and writer living in Brooklyn, New York, and the author of *Complete Embellishing*. You can find out more about her on thisisloveforever.com/blog.

(p. 148)

NICOLE VASBINDER is the designer behind Queen Puff Puff and is a proud member of the International Sisterhood of Seamsters. She recently opened StitchCraft, a sewing and craft studio in Petaluma, California.

(p. 105)

JESSICA WILSON is the mad photo-boothing mind behind scrumdillydilly.blogspot.com and scrumdillydo.blogspot.com. She is always in the middle of one project or another and distracts herself by baking goodies that taste scrumdillyumscious!

INDEX

Note: **Bold** page numbers indicate photos, and *italicized* page numbers indicate illustrations. (When only one number of a page range is bold or italicized, photos or illustrations appear on one or more of the pages.)

A

Accessories
  bags, 146–**51**
  hair, **136**–39
  See also Jewelry
Advanced projects
  handbags, 146–**49**
Amber Squares link bracelet, **89**
American history, 8–10, 12
Apron, 116–**17**
Architectural buttons, 12
Arlington, New Jersey, factory, **10**
Array of Buttons (jars), **156**
Art Deco styles, 9
Arts and Crafts movement, 9
Autumn Leaves Earrings, 84–**85**

B

Backstitch, *30*
Bags, 146–**51**
Bakelite buttons, 10, 13
Bakelite Cascading Earrings, **82**–83
Bakelite (haircomb), **138**–39
Bath set, **124**–25
Beading wire, *22*
Bead tips, *23*
Big-Eyed Owl (toy), **162**–63
Birds and Buttons Bag, 146–**47**
Blossom placemat, 118–**19**
Blue Array Earrings, 86–**87**
Bobby pins, **136**–37
Bone buttons, 13
Bracelets, 88–101
  charm, **90**–93
  cuffs, **94**–95
  knotted button, 96–**99**
  layered button, **100–101**
  link, **88**–89
Brass Cascading Earrings, **82**–83
British Empire, 9
Bronze Age, 6
Brooches, **104**–5
Burlap Buttons Necklace, 60–**71**
Button Blossom Pendant, 46–**47**
Button Bouquet Cards, 152–**53**
Button Collage, 132–**33**

Button Corsage, **140**
Button-Covered Band, **94**
Button Curve Necklace, 56–**57**
Button dangles, *26*
Button-making instructions, 15
Button Sampler Tote, **151**
Buttons and Beads Necklace, 54–55
Button shops, **7**, 11, 166
Button Tree, 160–**61**
Button weaving, *23*
Buttony Fabric Cuff, **95**
Buzzard Brand, 15

C

Cafe curtains, 110–13
Campaign buttons, 12
Canister, **157**
Cascading button earrings, **82**–83
Celluloid, 10
Center Sparkle Ring, **102**
Ceramic buttons, 13
Charm bracelets, **90**–93
Charm necklaces, 58–**61**
Charms, wineglass, **123**
Cheerful Flowers Curtains, **110**–11
Chokers, 50–**53**
Christmas decorations, 158–**61**
Circles and Blossoms Necklace, **62**–63
Circles and Curves Pendant, 44–**45**
Clam Cocktail Ring, **103**
Clothing, embellished, **140**–45
  See also Brooches
Collage, 132–**33**
Collecting, button, 9–10
Color Wheel Mirror, **130**–31
Costume jewelry, 12
Covered buttons, 13–14, *31–32*
  necklaces, 70–**73**
Crimp beads, *22*
Cuffs, **94**–95
Curtains, 110–**13**
Cutting off shanks, *28*

D

Daisy Magnets, 108–**9**
Dangle earrings, **80**–83
Dangles, *26*
Decor, home, 108–**33**
  bath set, **124**–25
  collage, 132–**33**
  curtains, **110**–13
  dinner party set, 122–**23**

kitchen set, 114–**17**
  magnets, 108–**9**
  mirror, 130–**31**
  pillows, 126–**29**
  table set, **118**–21
Decorations
  bags, 146–**51**
  clothing, **140**–45
  holiday, 158–**61**
  home, 164–**65**
  pillows, 126–**29**
Depictions on buttons, 8, 12
Dinner party set, 122–**23**
Dover, Ohio, museum, **14**
Drapes, 110–**13**
Drop earrings, 78–**79**
Dual Lines Pendant, **40**
Duo pendants, **40**, **41**

E

Early America, 8
Earrings, 76–**87**
  dangle, **80**–83
  drop, **78**–79
  hoop, 84–**87**
  post, 76–**77**
Easthampton, Massachusetts, shop, **7**
Easy projects
  bags, **150**–51
  bath set, **124**–25
  brooches, **104**–5
  button cuff, **94**
  button link necklace, 62–63
  chokers, **50**–53
  covered button necklaces, 70–**73**
  curtains, 112–**13**
  dangle earrings, **80**–83
  dinner party set, 122–**23**
  drop earrings, 78–**79**
  duo pendants, **40**, **41**
  embellishments, **140**–45
  hair clips, **136**–37
  haircomb, **138**–39
  holiday decoration, 158–**59**
  hoop earrings, 86–**87**
  jars, **156**–57
  kitchen set, 114–**17**
  layered pendant, 44–**45**
  link bracelets, **88**–89
  magnets, 108–**9**
  mirror, 130–**31**
  pillow, 128–**29**
  post earrings, 76–**77**

rings, **102**–3
skirts, embellished, 142–**45**
solo pendants, **38**, **39**
table set, **118**–21
tote bags, **150–51**
wreath, 158–**59**
Embellishments
  bags, **146**–51
  clothing, **140**–45
  history, 8–10, 12
  pillows, 126–**29**
Enamel buttons, 14
Essex Pearl Button Factory, **10**
Exclusive Buttons, 11

F

Factory, button, **10**
Filigree Flowers Earrings, **81**
Findings, 166
First Golden Age, **6**–8
Flirty Skirt, **142**–43
Flower Clips, **137**
Flower Garden Hand Towel, **124**–25
Flower Loop Washcloth, **124**–25
Four Seasons Napkin Rings, 120–**21**
Frog buttons, 14

G

Gifts, 152–**65**
Glass buttons, 14
Glendale and Nashawannuck, **7**
Glossy Reds and Pinks Bracelet, **90**–91
Gluing
  materials, 33
  techniques, *34*
Grab Bag Magnets, 108–**9**
Great Depression, 9–10
Greece, Ancient, 6

H

Hair accessories
  clips, **136**–37
  combs, **138**–39
Handbags, 146–**49**
Hand towel, **124**–25
Historical buttons, 13
History of buttons, **6–10**, 12
Hobby of collecting, 9–10
Holiday decorations, 158–**61**
Hoop earrings, 84–**87**
Horn buttons, 16
Housewares, 108–**33**
  bath set, **124**–25
  collage, 132–**33**

curtains, **110**–13
dinner party set, **122–23**
kitchen set, 114–**17**
magnets, 108–**9**
mirror, **130**–31
pillows, 126–**29**
table set, **118**–21

I

Indians, American, 8
Initialed Pillow, 126–**27**
International trade, 7
Ivory buttons, 16

J

Jars, **156–57**
Jet buttons, 16
Jewelry
  bracelets, **88**–101
  brooches, **104–5**
  earrings, 76–**87**
  materials, 20–**22**, 166
  necklaces, 52–**53**
  rings, **102–3**
  techniques, 22–28
Jump rings, 27

K

Kitchen set, 114–**17**
Knotted button bracelets, 96–**99**
Knotting, 22

L

Layered button bracelets,
  100–101
Leather buttons, 16
Link bracelets, **88–89**
Linked Up Pendant, **41**
Lithographed buttons, 12
Long and Low Flowers Earrings,
  80
Loop-D-Loops (curtains), 112–**13**
Looping, wire, 27

M

Machine sewing, 32
Magnets, 108–**9**
Making buttons, 15
Map of United States, **8**
Market bag, **150**
Massachusetts button shop, 7
Mass production of buttons, 6–8
Materials
  buttons, 11, 13–**17**
  jewelry-making, 20–**22**
  sewing, 28
Metal buttons, 16
Middle Ages, 6
Military buttons, 9

Mirror, **130**–31
Mod Deluxe Pendant, 48–**49**
Moderately hard projects
  bags, 146–**51**
  button charm necklaces, 58–**61**
  button link necklaces, 62–**65**
  charm bracelets, **90–93**
  Christmas tree, 160–**61**
  collage, 132–**33**
  covered button necklaces,
    70–**73**
  curtains, 110–**13**
  decorations, 164–**65**
  delicate pendants, 46–**49**
  duo pendant, **40**
  fabric cuff, **95**
  haircomb, **138**–39
  handbags, 146–**49**
  holiday decoration, 160–**61**
  hoop earrings, 84–**85**
  knotted button bracelets, 96–**99**
  knotted necklaces, 66–**69**
  layered button bracelets,
    100–101
  layered pendant, 42–**43**
  pillow, 126–**27**
  row of buttons necklaces, 54–57
  stationery set, 152–**55**
  tote bags, **150–51**
  toys, 162–**63**
Molly's Button Skirt, 144–**45**
Museum, button, **14**

N

Napkin rings, 120–**21**
Napkins, **122**
Native Americans, 8
Necklaces, 38–73
  button charm, 58–**61**
  button link, 62–**65**
  chokers, 50–**53**
  covered button, 70–**73**
  knotted, 66–**69**
  row of buttons, 54–**57**
  See also Pendants
New Jersey button factory, **10**

O

Ohio button museum, **14**
Oven mitt, 114–**15**

P

Pearlescent Necklace, 68–**69**
Pencil Canister with Button Mag-
  nets, **157**
Pencil cup, 154–**55**
Pendants
  delicate, 46–**49**

duo, **40, 41**
  layered, **42–45**
  solo, **38, 39**
"Picture" buttons, 12
Pillows, 126–**29**
Pink and Gold Deluxe (embellish-
  ment), **140**
Pink Rounds Link Bracelet, **88**
Placemat, **118**–19
Plastic buttons, 16
Political buttons, 8, 12
Polka Dots Galore (pillow),
  128–**29**
Post earrings, 76–**77**
Pot holder, 114–**15**
Pretty in Pink Earrings, **78**
Pretty Pencil Cup, 154–**55**
Purses, 146–**49**

R

"Realistics," 10–12, 13
Red and Gold Bracelet, **101**
Red and Gold Wreath, 158–**59**
Red Bird Brooch, **104**
Red Dashes and Dots Necklace,
  58–**59**
Red Rounds Earrings, 76–**77**
Renaissance, 6
Rings, **102–3**
Rome, Ancient, 6
Row of Sparkles (haircomb),
  138–39

S

Semiprecious buttons, 17
Sew Cute Apron, 116–**17**
Sewing
  button, 29, 29–30
  machine, 32
  materials, 28
  techniques, 29–32
Sewing Revolution, 9–10
Sew-through buttons, 17, 29
Shades of Gray Evening Bag,
  148–**49**
Shank buttons, 17, 29
Shanks, cutting off, 28
Shining Silver Charm Bracelet,
  92–**93**
Shiny Set (hair clips), **136**
Shiraz Necklace, 66–**67**
Shopping for buttons, **7**, 11, 166
Silver Spotlight Earrings, **79**
Skirts, embellished, **142**–45
Solo pendants, **38, 39**
Sparkle Pop Pendant, **39**
Spiky Button Chokers, **50**–53

Spring Roll Delight (market bag),
  150
Springtime Mix Bracelet, **100**
Stationery set, 152–**55**
Stokes, Laura, 15
Stone Age, 6
Stone buttons, 17
"Story" buttons, 12
Stuffed toy, **162–63**
Styles of buttons, 12–13
Sunny Days Necklace, 60–**61**
Supplies, 11, 20–**22**, 166

T

Table set, **118**–21
Tender Buttons, 11
Timeline of buttons, **6–10**, 12
Tools, jewelry, 20–**22**, 166
Tops, embellished, **140–41**
  See also Brooches
Towels, **124–25**
Toys, **162–63**
Tree, Christmas, 160–**61**
Triple Dip Feedsack Necklace,
  72–**73**
Types of buttons, 17, 29

U

Under the Sea Bracelet, **98–99**
U.S. history, 8–10, 12

V

Vegetable ivory buttons, 17
Vintage buttons, **6–10**, 12
  See also Supplies
Vintage Costume Earrings, 76–**77**
Vintage Flower Pendant, **38**
Vintage Flowers Necklace, 64–**65**
Vintage Sparkle Brooch, **105**
Vinyl pendant, 42–**43**

W

War of 1812, 9
Warther's Button Museum, **14**
Washcloth, **124–25**
Weaving, 23
Wineglass charms, **123**
Wire looping, 27
Wood buttons, 17
Wood Dual Drop Choker, 52–**53**
Wooden Rounds Bracelet, 96–**97**
Woodland Fairy (decoration),
  164–**65**
World War II, 10
Wrapped loops, 25
Wreath, 158–**59**

Z

Zigzag Oven Mitt, 114–**15**